abt

WORLD WAR I

HISTORY OF WARFARE

Donald Sommerville

RSVP

RAINTREE
STECK-VAUGHN
PUBLISHERS
A Steck-Vaughn Company

Austin, Texas

www.steck-vaughn.com

Steck-Vaughn Company

First published 1999 by Raintree Steck-Vaughn Publishers,
an imprint of Steck-Vaughn Company.
Copyright © 1999 Brown Partworks Limited.

Library of Congress Cataloging-in-Publication Data

Sommerville, Donald,   (1957–
    World War I.
        p.   cm. — (History of warfare)
    Includes bibliographical references and index.
    Summary: Examines the causes, course, and social implications of World War I, as well as technological and strategic advances of the time.
    ISBN 0 8172-5450-1
    1. World War I, 1914–18--Juvenile literature.   2. Military art and science--Juvenile literature.   3. Military history, Modern--20th century--Juvenile literature.   [1. World War, 1914–18]
    I. Title.   II. Series: History of warfare (Austin, Tex.)
    D522.7.S66   1999
    940.3--dc21   98-39037
                                                                     CIP
                                                                     AC

Printed and bound in the United States
1 2 3 4 5 6 7 8 9 0 IP 03 02 01 00 99 98

Brown Partworks Limited
Managing Editor: Ian Westwell
Senior Designer: Paul Griffin
Picture Researcher: Wendy Verren
Editorial Assistant: Antony Shaw
Cartographer: William le Bihan
Index: Pat Coward

Raintree Steck-Vaughn
Publishing Director: Walter Kossmann
Project Manager: Joyce Spicer
Editor: Shirley Shalit

Front cover: German dead litter the ground in front of a French machine gun, 1918 (main picture) and French soldier charges into battle, 1914 (inset).
Page 1: U.S. troops in action during the fighting around Château-Thierry, France, in 1918.

Consultant
Dr. Niall Barr, Senior Lecturer,
Royal Military Academy Sandhurst,
Camberley, Surrey, England

Acknowledgments listed on page 80 constitute part of this copyright page.

CONTENTS

INTRODUCTION

World War I, fought between 1914 and 1918, was a conflict that heralded the dawn of modern warfare. Huge armies battled in many parts of the world on land, at sea, and for the first time in military history, in the air. The war also saw a massive increase in the power of weapons. Technology and industrial output became the keys to success on the battlefield. Victory no longer depended on soldiers alone, but on the ability of their civilians and industries at home to provide them with the huge number of weapons and supplies needed to continue the fight.

Few generals or politicians really understood the power of the new weapons, and the huge casualties of the war showed, in part, that they never found a way to reduce their consequences. At the beginning of the war, soldiers went into battle using tactics that had changed little in 50 years, but the weapons they faced had been changed almost beyond recognition over the same period. Artillery had a longer range and greater accuracy than ever before.

On land, once the war of movement had ended and trench warfare began, the defending generals had all the advantages. Trenches, barbed wire, machine guns, and artillery could smash an attack. Military leaders tried many ways to break through the lines of trenches. Long and short pre-attack artillery barrages lasting days or just hours, poison gas, and tanks were all used, with limited success, to defeat the enemy. Even if a large gap was made in an enemy's trenches, it was rarely exploited because of the difficulties of getting more troops forward quickly across shell-blasted terrain. Horses were still the main means of transport, although transportation powered by the internal combustion engine was being slowly introduced.

At sea, the large armored battleship remained the chief weapon, but there was only one major battle between rival fleets during the war. Both sides knew that to lose all their best ships gambling on victory in one battle would have been disastrous. However, the naval war was crucial, and a new weapon, the submarine, began to play a key role in naval warfare. Submarines were used to sink enemy warships and, more importantly, to attack enemy supply ships. The war at sea also saw the beginnings of naval aviation. Early aircraft carriers were developed, although they had a very limited effect.

The importance of aircraft was not really understood in 1914. They were used for target spotting or reporting on enemy movements at the start. However, by the end of the conflict aircraft were used on long-range bombing missions, in support of ground attacks, and as fighters.

Germany lost World War I for three reasons. First, it was starved into defeat because of a naval blockade. Second, its armies were bled white because of the huge casualties they suffered. Third, the United States, with all its manpower and industrial might, entered the war in 1917. Against such resources, Germany's generals could never hope to win the war.

THE RIVALS AND THEIR PLANS

In 1914, when World War I started, leaders in many countries thought that the only way they could be successful was to compete with their neighbors. They wanted their countries to grow strong and rich. Many of them thought that the best way to do this was to be prepared to grab what they wanted from other countries and if necessary to fight wars to do so. Powerful nations in Europe also formed protective alliances with each other, leaving the continent divided between two vast power blocs that did not trust each other.

Although it soon involved countries and peoples from virtually every continent on the Earth, World War I began mainly as a European conflict. The United States was the only country outside Europe that ranked as a major world power, but in 1914 most Americans preferred to stay out of Europe's quarrels. America would not join the war until 1917.

The assassination of Austria's Archduke Ferdinand on June 28, 1914. His death led to Europe being plunged into World War I.

Powerful European rivals

The map of Europe in 1914 was very different from that of today. There were five "great powers" at the time: Germany, Austria-Hungary, France, Russia, and Britain. The five powers had formed two opposing alliances—Germany and Austria-Hungary, known as the Central Powers, were on one side; opposing them were Britain, France, and Russia, known as the Entente (or Allies). These countries were economic rivals, many were also carving out overseas empires, and the majority had potentially huge armies supplied by vast armament industries. These factors led the two power blocs to be very suspicious of each other. Their rivalries needed just one event for them to go to war.

Under their military systems peacetime armies were only a proportion of the size they would become in war. To get to their full strength, armies needed to mobilize.

German troops march into Belgium at the beginning of World War I, August 1914. Within a few months, the war became bogged down in the static trench warfare that was to last until the final weeks of the war. The line of trenches in Western Europe, which stretched from the North Sea through Belgium and France to Switzerland, was known as the Western Front.

That is to say they had to call back reservists (men who had had compulsory military training) from civilian life, give them guns and equipment, and move them to the war zone. This took time. No one wanted to risk letting their opponents start the process first in case they would lose the war before they had their army ready. This meant that, once one country started mobilizing, everyone else would.

Germany's generals took this reasoning a stage further. They did not think they could hold out against the full strength of the Russian and French armies, but they knew that the Russians would take longer to get ready. The Germans planned to attack France first with most of their army. France, they thought, would be beaten before Russia was ready. The Germans could then move against Russia without having to fight a long war on two fronts. This strategy meant that the German army would immediately start attacking France. This plan was devised by General Alfred von Schlieffen.

The war begins

What happened in 1914 was that Austria-Hungary, Germany, and Russia became involved in a minor quarrel over Serbia, a small country in southeast Europe friendly to Russia. A member of Austria-Hungary's royal family, Archduke Franz Ferdinand, was assassinated in Serbia on June 28. Austria-Hungary used the event as a reason to declare war on Serbia on July 28. Then the system of alliances kicked in; one by one the members of the rival alliances declared war on each other. Germany saw the assassination as an excuse to go to war, and was particularly eager to capture valuable coalfields along either side of the French and Belgian border. By August 6, Austria-Hungary and Germany were at war with Britain, France, Russia, and Serbia.

By the 6th, Germany had already launched an attack against France through Belgium and Luxembourg. The unrealistic part of the so-called "Schlieffen Plan" was that, to protect themselves against Russia, Germany's generals thought they had no option but to attack France—and the sooner they did it the better since a lead of even a day or two in the race to mobilize could mean the difference between victory and total defeat.

GERMANY'S WAR PLANS

In the 60 years before 1914 the German army became the most powerful in Europe. The secret of its success was the creation of a highly efficient General Staff, which tried to run the army by precise rules. Count Alfred von Schlieffen was Chief of the General Staff from 1891 to 1905, and the war plan he devised was still the basis of German strategy in 1914.

The so-called "Schlieffen Plan" would not have been possible without Germany's well-developed railroad system. The plan laid down to the minute how many hundreds of troop trains would move German soldiers against France as soon as the French mobilized. Germany's generals told their politicians that stopping the plan once it had started would lead to such chaos that they would lose the war.

There were three problems with all this. First, the German generals assumed that it was morally acceptable to get what they wanted from other countries by force. Second, their ideas meant that Germany's national policy was dictated by their military plans, and not the other, more sensible, way around where military plans are devised to fit national interests. Finally, they were completely wrong when they thought that events in a war could be exactly, even mathematically, planned or predicted. They tried to run their war as precisely as their train timetables. Events soon proved that "war by timetable" was impossible.

Count Alfred von Schlieffen, the creator of Germany's attack on France in 1914.

Many leaders in most European countries wanted to go to war, but they knew it was a very serious thing to do. Some might have tried harder to stay at peace, but their generals told them this was dangerous. Germany's generals were the worst of all; their plans ensured that virtually the whole of Europe would soon be involved in the conflict.

FIRST MOVES IN THE WEST

France and Germany were the most powerful countries in Europe in 1914 and the major military theater throughout the war became the so-called Western Front. It was here, from the North Sea to Switzerland, where the most important parts of their two armies fought. The French were soon joined by most of Britain's army and later by other Entente—or Allied—forces as well. The war began with both sides moving rapidly, but by Christmas 1914 the rivals had begun to dig trenches along the Western Front.

France's war plan in 1914 was called Plan XVII. Its aim was to get revenge for the humiliating defeat France had suffered at Germany's hands in the Franco-Prussian War of 1870–71, and to recover the territory in Alsace and Lorraine on France's eastern border that Germany had captured then. France called up about 1.3 million troops in five armies, and the strategy was to send three of these into furious all-out attacks to recapture the lost territory.

France's commander-in-chief, General Joseph Joffre, realized that Germany might try to outflank his forces by moving into France from the north through Belgium. He held his other two armies in reserve to guard against this. However, the French underestimated the total size of the German forces and did not understand what percentage of the total German strength would be deployed against them. They thought the Germans

Belgian civilians look on as German troops march through Brussels. The Belgian capital had been captured on August 20 during the early stages of the German offensive against France. Belgium's small army could do nothing to halt the progress of the invaders.

would have to leave more troops in the east to fight Russia, but instead almost two million German troops attacked France out of their total army of 2.4 million men.

Germany's war plan was the Schlieffen Plan (see page 7), now to be executed by his successor, General Helmuth von Moltke. Schlieffen's idea was to concentrate so much of Germany's army on the right wing (close to Belgium) that it would quickly over-run northern France, capture Paris, the French capital, and then swing around behind the main French forces in Alsace to the south. It was a risky strategy. Even before the war, Moltke had shown that he might not have the nerve to stick with it. The key right wing in the north was still the strongest part of the German forces but, while Schlieffen had wanted it to consist of 90 percent of his men, Moltke had cut its share back to 60 percent.

Rapid German gains

The Schlieffen Plan began with a German advance into Belgium. Belgium wanted to stay out of any war between the Great Powers. Germany's leaders did not care about this and attacked anyway. Britain had been friendly with France and Belgium before the war and this attack on them made the British furious with the Germans, ensuring that the British would join in the war on the side of France and Russia, which they did on August 4.

The Germans began the sweep into Belgium on August 3, 1914. They quickly pushed the small Belgian army aside, using massive new artillery guns to smash the Belgian border fortress at Liège. They captured Brussels, the Belgian capital, on the 20th. The British and the two reserve French armies tried to stop them in battles in the Ardennes area and along the border between Belgium and France. The Germans came off best in all these battles and the Allied forces had to retreat southward into France.

In the meantime other French armies had been trying to carry out Plan XVII, but attacks in Alsace and Lorraine failed. Now the Germans were advancing in these sectors, too, and Moltke decided to water down the Schlieffen Plan even more. He sent forces to strengthen the attacks in Alsace and took more troops away from his right wing and sent them east to face the Russians.

The greatest problem for the two commanders-in-chief was to work out exactly where their frontline troops were. With millions of men spread across an area covering hundreds of miles, the old-fashioned horse messengers could not do the job properly, but the commanders had to make do with them. Joffre had a better

THE FRENCH AT WAR

Germany had a larger population than France. The puzzle for France's top generals in 1914 was to find a winning strategy that would counteract this superiority in numbers.

Napoleon Bonaparte, France's greatest soldier, had believed that the will to win was the essential ingredient of battlefield success. This was correct, as far as it went, but in 1914 France's generals thought it was the only way to achieve what they wanted. They developed the idea to ridiculous extremes and taught their soldiers that attacking at every opportunity was the certain route to victory. They did not think that the firepower of enemy artillery and machine guns might make a more systematic approach more successful and reduce the likelihood of heavy casualties.

One of the leading teachers of the systematic and more cautious approach to war was General Ferdinand Foch who was a professor at France's War College before the war. He commanded part of the French army in 1914, with more success than some other French generals, but was sidelined for a time when French plans changed. In 1918, however, Foch was brought in as commander-in-chief of all the British and French armies in France. In this role he played a vital part in the final victory.

French troops charge a German position at the beginning of the war. Such attacks in the face of massive firepower led to enormous French casualties in 1914.

idea of where his own troops and their enemies were than Moltke. This gave the Allies a crucial advantage over the Germans in the next phase of the campaign.

By the start of September, the Allied armies had retreated from northern France almost as far as Paris, but a large gap had appeared in the German line. The French had assembled new reserve forces and knew where this weak gap was. In the Battle of the Marne, between September 5 and 10, French and British troops eventually forced the Germans to retreat.

The Allied victory in the Battle of the Marne meant that the Schlieffen Plan had failed. Although the Germans had overrun a large part of northern France and the small British army had been virtually destroyed, the fight would go on. Instead of knocking France out of the war in a few weeks of fighting, the German generals would have to face their nightmare of a war in the west against France and Britain and another in the east against Russia. Moltke was fired because of the failure of the Schlieffen Plan. His replacement was General Erich von Falkenhayn.

The "Race to the Sea"

Although the Battle of the Marne had been decisive, it did not mean that the fighting in France was over for the year. The two sets of armies were now concentrated in eastern France, north of Paris, but there were few troops between these positions and the English Channel to the northwest. Both sides now tried to maneuver around the north end of their opponent's line, aiming to outflank their opponent. Each time they tried this maneuver, they ran straight into enemy forces trying to do the same thing in the opposite direction.

From late September through November vicious but indecisive battles were fought along the Aisne River, then in the Artois and Picardy regions of northern France, and finally in southern Belgium around the city of Ypres. These increasingly desperate attempts to find the enemy's open flank by both sides became

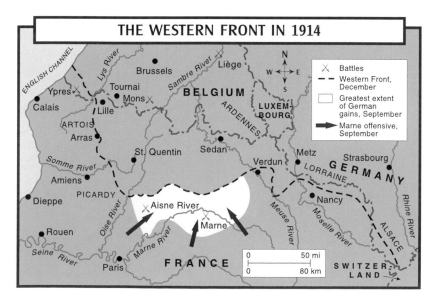

THE WESTERN FRONT IN 1914

The German generals believed they could conquer France in a matter of weeks in 1914. When their initial plan failed, the war of movement ended and both sides began to dig in.

known as the "Race to the Sea." Neither side won the race to find an open flank. The year came to an end with the exhausted armies digging in along a continuous 400-mile (640-km) front that stretched from the English Channel in the north to the Swiss border in the south.

The generals of both sides, neither of which had expected the war to last more than a few months, had to take stock of the situation. Their armies were exhausted, they were short of winter clothing and supplies, and there seemed no obvious and quick way of winning the war before the end of the winter of 1914–15.

THE BRITISH ARMY

Britain was the exception among the European countries in 1914. Every other country tried to give most of its young men some military training and planned to recall them for service in huge "citizen armies" in time of war. Britain relied instead on a smaller force of professional regular soldiers. Britain's soldiers were very well trained, but many of them were killed in the first few months of World War I.

By the end of 1914 the British realized that the war would last more than a few months. Britain's generals knew that it would be necessary to expand the army. However, the casualties and the small original size of the force meant that it took nearly two years for the British to assemble a large and efficient army.

Britain's army in France was known as the British Expeditionary Force (B.E.F.). It was commanded throughout 1914 and 1915 by General Sir John French. He wanted to do what he could to help defend France against German attack, but he also had to remember that if he got into trouble he could lose virtually all of Britain's experienced soldiers.

Members of a British cavalry regiment rest during the "Race to the Sea," October 1914.

While the generals retired to their various headquarters to plan a renewal of the war in the spring of 1915, the soldiers left to defend their respective front lines throughout the winter recognized that the bloody battles of the previous summer and fall were likely to continue in the new year. So they took matters into their own hands.

The Christmas truce

On Christmas Day 1914, at certain points along the Western Front, the bitter enemies of the previous summer and fall climbed out of their trenches under flags of truce to exchange gifts, including tobacco, alcohol, and chocolate. It was a gesture from the past. Ordinary soldiers, as much as their commanders, were still unaware of the full horror of modern industrial war.

In August 1914 soldiers on both sides had hoped that the war would be "over by Christmas." Many had fought with enthusiasm at first, seeing the war as both just and patriotic and a means to escape a dull civilian life. By the end of the year such optimistic thoughts were buried in the freezing mud of the trenches and the massive casualties of four terrible months of modern war. Almost a million men had already been killed or wounded on each side, and another four years of bloody fighting lay ahead.

British and German troops pictured during one of the many unauthorized truces that took place at Christmas 1914. The meetings took place in no-man's-land, the area between the lines of trenches.

Halting the Russians

World War I began with a quarrel between Austria-Hungary and Serbia. Austria-Hungary was therefore faced with a smaller version of Germany's "war on two fronts" problem, but against Serbia in the south and against Russia, Serbia's ally, in what is now Poland and the Ukraine in the north and east. Russia declared war on Austria-Hungary on August 1, 1914. The war on the Eastern Front began badly for Germany and Austria-Hungary, but the two powers recovered quickly to launch new attacks.

Austro-Hungarian troops watch over Russian prisoners captured during the opening stages of the war on the Eastern Front in 1914. However, it was the German army that won the greatest victories in the campaign.

Austria-Hungary's chief-of-staff, General Franz Conrad von Hötzendorf, could not decide which front should have priority. Austria-Hungary was defeated in both sectors in 1914. The outnumbered Serbs fought the Austro-Hungarians to a standstill in August and September 1914, while the Russians were overrunning much of the Austro-Hungarian province of Galicia.

Farther north still, where the Germans and Russians fought, it was a different story. In an attempt to help their ally France, the Russians attacked the German province of East Prussia in August but were beaten by the Germans in the Battle of Tannenberg. The Russians were not discouraged by this setback and tried to restart their offensive. This time they aimed to strike farther

south, from Russia's Polish territories into the German area of Silesia. The Russian attack was halted by a German advance around Lódz in November. Many of the German troops had been brought to the sector by railroad.

Austria-Hungary was defeated by the Russians in the first part of 1915. The Austro-Hungarian fortress of Przemysl surrendered. Moltke had been fired as German chief-of-staff in 1914 when the Schlieffen Plan failed in France, and he was replaced by General Erich von Falkenhayn. Falkenhayn wanted to concentrate on the Western Front but, after the Austro-Hungarian defeats, the German emperor, Wilhelm II, ordered him to give the Eastern Front priority. With the troops he sent east, the Germans attacked.

The German and Austro-Hungarian armies began their

THE EASTERN FRONT IN 1914–15

Battles

Borders, 1914

Front line, December 1915

0   200 mi

0   300 km

offensive around the towns of Gorlice and Tarnow in Galicia in May 1915. By the start of June the Germans had broken through. The Russians called it the "great retreat," and it did not stop until the bad weather of the fall. By then the Germans had advanced over 300 miles (480 km). Czar Nicholas II, the Russian ruler, fired his top commander and took charge himself.

In the fighting in 1915 the Russian armies lost about one million men killed and wounded, and another million taken prisoner. Late in 1915 there was more success for Russia's enemies. Bulgaria joined in the war on the Central Powers' side and helped in a final offensive that ended the stubborn Serbian resistance. Serbia was completely defeated during October and November. The Central Powers' successes in 1915 were not cheaply won, however. Together, Germany and Austria-Hungary had about one million casualties on the Eastern Front.

The war on the Eastern Front in 1914 remained much more open than on the Western Front. The huge distances involved guaranteed that the lines of trenches seen in the west were much rarer.

FAILURE AT GALLIPOLI

The Ottoman Empire, based in Turkey, had entered the war on the German side in October 1914. This had closed the supply route from the western Allies to Russia through the Mediterranean and Black Seas. Without supplies of guns and munitions from Britain and France, Russia's huge armies were left struggling on the Eastern Front. The British and French needed to find a way to open the Dardanelles, a Turkish-controlled channel linking the eastern Mediterranean with the Black Sea, to get equipment to the Russians.

British artillerymen fire on one of the Turkish positions on the high ground that surrounded the main Allied landing beaches on the Gallipoli Peninsula.

At the start of 1915 Britain's navy minister, Winston Churchill, convinced other Allied leaders to attack Turkey, aiming to reopen the supply route to Russia and knock Germany's weakest partner out of the war. The Allies at first hoped that their ships could do the job on their own. They sent a fleet to bombard Turkish forts on either side of the Dardanelles in February.

This operation seemed to go quite well so the Allied ships returned on March 18 for a full-scale attack. Many of the Turkish guns were knocked out and, though the Allies did not know it, the Turkish guns still undamaged were running out of ammunition. It might only have taken a little longer for the Allied ships to sail to the Turkish capital, Constantinople (now Istanbul), and force the Turks to surrender. However, four Allied battleships suddenly struck mines and sank. The naval attack was called off.

The Allies now decided to invade the Gallipoli Peninsula on the north side of the Dardanelles and advance by that land route to the Turkish capital. Unfortunately for the Allies it took weeks to get the invasion force ready. The Turks used the time to rush troops to the area. When the Allies began landing on April 25, the Turks had managed to assemble just enough troops to stop them, helped by poor leadership and organization on the Allied side.

The Allied troops, many of whom were from Australia and New Zealand, soon found that what had been planned as a great strategic maneuver turned into a version of the Western Front, but with worse terrain and few alternatives to frontal attacks on tough enemy positions placed on hills overlooking the Allied trenches.

THE GALLIPOLI CAMPAIGN

The landings abandoned

The Allies tried to restart their advance by making landings on an additional beachhead in August. The Turks were surprised, but poor British leadership again destroyed the slim chances of success. One unit even stopped to have breakfast halfway up a crucial hill. By the time they were ready to move on, the Turks had stationed troops at the top and the British could not capture it.

A new British commander took over in October and recommended that the landing force be evacuated. Pulling out under the noses of the Turks was a very dangerous operation but it was brilliantly planned and carried out. No Allied lives were lost during the two-stage withdrawal in December 1915 and January 1916. However, in the earlier fighting each side had suffered about 250,000 casualties.

The Gallipoli campaign was a daring plan that might have knocked Turkey out of the war. However, poor Allied planning allowed the Turks to overcome their initial surprise and pin the Allies on their landing sites.

EGYPT AND PALESTINE

In 1914 the Ottoman Empire governed the whole of the Middle East from Turkey in the north to the Arabian Peninsula in the south and Iraq in the east. Before World War I the Ottoman Empire had been known as the "sick man of Europe" because it had been so inefficiently run. The Arab peoples of the region resented the way they were bossed around by the Turks who ruled the empire. Britain and France thought this gave them the opportunity to extend their empires at the expense of the Turks.

Turkish troops march through a village during their opening attack against the British in Egypt, January 1915.

British forces had occupied Egypt for many years before the war to protect the Suez Canal, which was a vital link in the route between Britain and the British Empire territories in India, Australia, and New Zealand. Turkey declared war in October 1914 as its rulers feared the Russians. The Suez Canal was the target for the first Turkish attack. In January 1915, 20,000

WAR IN THE MIDDLE EAST

BLACK SEA

Constantinople

RUSSIAN EMPIRE

TURKEY

OTTOMAN EMPIRE

CASPIAN SEA

Aleppo

MEDITERRANEAN SEA

SYRIA

Megiddo 1918

Jerusalem 1917

PERSIA

Damascus

Gaza

Romani 1916

Beersheba 1917

Suez Canal

SINAI DESERT

ARABIA

Aqaba 1917

EGYPT

Gulf of Aqaba

Battles

0   300 mi

0   400 km

N
W ← → E
S

RED SEA

Mecca

BAHRAIN

PERSIAN GULF

The fighting in the Middle East was much more fluid and open than on the Western Front, chiefly because of the vast distances involved. Cavalry and motorized transport, as well as aircraft, played vital roles in the final British victory.

Turkish soldiers crossed the 100 miles (160 km) of the waterless Sinai Desert from Palestine to Egypt. Because they aimed to cross the Suez Canal, they even carried boats with them all the way. It was a waste of effort. When they attacked on February 2, the British defenders easily beat them off and they had to retreat.

Hit-and-run warfare

Because of their commitments in other areas, neither side did much on this front until the summer of 1916, when the British began an advance across the Sinai Desert. The advance was very slow because the troops had to build a water pipeline and a rail-road to carry their supplies as they went. There was one impor-tant battle, at Romani in August 1916, in which a Turkish attack on the Allied advance was badly defeated. By early 1917 the British had advanced nearly to Gaza in Palestine.

In the meantime two other contending forces had come onto the scene, one on each side in the war. In June 1916 many of the Arab people living in what is now Saudi Arabia rose up against

Indian cavalrymen, part of the British forces fighting in Egypt and Palestine, pursue the retreating Turkish troops after the Battle of Beersheba in late October 1917.

their Turkish overlords. They quickly captured the holy city of Mecca and attacked many Turkish outposts. The British sent guns and advisers to help them, especially T.E. Lawrence, known as "Lawrence of Arabia." Lawrence and the principal Arab leader, Faisal ibn Husayn, led the Arab forces in a daring and successful attack on the port of Aqaba, on the Gulf of Aqaba, in July 1917. From this new base the Arabs continued their hit-and-run attacks on isolated Turkish garrisons and their long lines of communication throughout Arabia and southern Palestine.

From late 1915 into early 1917 British forces in Egypt faced a new enemy, the Senussi, a Muslim group from North Africa. In December 1915 the Senussi invaded Egypt from the west. The British used cavalry and armored cars fitted with machine guns to counteract the Senussi's desert mobility, winning a battle against them in February 1916. The Senussi next fought a guerrilla campaign, launching hit-and-run attacks and ambushes but avoiding large-scale battles. The Senussi tied down over 100,000 Allied troops before making peace in April 1917.

On to Jerusalem

By March 1917 the British thought they were ready to break into Palestine on the main battlefront. They attacked along the coast near Gaza on March 26. The attack went very well at first. The Turkish forces were surrounded and on the verge of retreat— then the British general foolishly withdrew some of his men. The Turks recovered, won the battle, and then defeated a second British attack the next month. The British government knew that their generals should have done better. They fired them and sent out General Edmund Allenby. Allenby's orders were to capture Jerusalem by Christmas and he did just that.

Allenby built up his forces over the summer and planned a daring attack for October. Instead of moving along the coast once again, he would strike inland near Beersheba, southwest of Jerusalem. It was a very risky plan because the Turks held all the best water sources in this desert area. The British would have to capture them in the first hours of the battle or their troops, and the horses and camels of their cavalry, might die of thirst. Secrecy was absolutely vital if the attack was to get off to this essential good start.

Allenby's careful planning paid off. The attackers captured Beersheba on October 31. The Turkish army had to retreat, and Allenby and his men entered Jerusalem on December 8. After that the advance came to a stop for some months because Allenby had to send some of his units back to the Western Front in Europe to help against the German attacks in France in the spring and summer of 1918.

The Turks defeated

By the late summer of 1918 Allenby was ready to advance once again. The result was another major victory in the Battle of Megiddo on September 19. One Turkish army was destroyed, and a second was forced into a headlong retreat. The victorious Allied army reached Damascus, capital of Syria, on October 1, entering the city at almost the same time as Lawrence and the Arab guerrilla forces.

By the last weeks of the month the Allied advance had reached Aleppo in northern Syria. On October 30, Turkey surrendered. In little more than a month Allenby had advanced 360 miles (576 km), capturing 350 Turkish artillery guns and vast amounts of other war supplies.

The Arab forces had played a vital part in this final Allied success. Although the British forces won the big battles, four times as many Turkish troops were involved in fighting the Arab guerrillas or protecting the outlying parts of the Ottoman Empire against their attacks as were engaged against Allenby's men.

THE BATTLE OF MEGIDDO

The Allied victory in Palestine in September 1918 is known as the Battle of Megiddo. Like General Edmund Allenby's success at Beersheba the year before, it began with a surprise attack. By leaked information the Turks were fooled into thinking the Allied cavalry would be relaxing off duty and that they would be holding a race meet the day the attack was to begin.

Instead, on September 19, a British artillery bombardment smashed the Turkish frontline positions near the coast. An infantry attack then opened up a gap, and the Allied cavalry raced through, throwing the Turkish troops into a panic.

The Turkish generals and their German allies never had a chance of pulling their forces together as British air attacks on their headquarters, communication lines, and road and rail junctions added to the confusion.

Thousands of Turks were bombed and machine-gunned, trapped in the region's narrow valleys. Many quickly surrendered. Over 75,000 Turks were taken prisoner between the start of the battle and the end of the war in this theater. No one knows how many more were killed, but the Allied force suffered fewer than 1,000 men killed.

THE WAR IN ITALY

Italy was officially allied with Germany and Austria-Hungary when World War I broke out in 1914, but the Italian government decided to remain neutral for the moment. However, many people living in the Austro-Hungarian border areas were Italian-speaking. Some Italian leaders wanted to capture these territories and unite them with the rest of Italy. This was why Italy did not keep to its alliance with Austria-Hungary in 1914 and why, in May 1915, the Italians joined the Allies and declared war on Austria-Hungary.

Italian mountain troops, known as Alpini, prepare to launch a surprise attack on the Austro-Hungarians in the Trentino Mountains.

The Austro-Hungarian forces were already fighting against Russia and Serbia, so for the remainder of 1915 they did not attempt any major attacks against the Italians. Instead they tried only to hold on to their border defenses. The Italians did all the attacking in the northeast of their country, along the disputed border region with Austria-Hungary.

Italian setbacks

The fighting took place in two regions: in the Trentino district, north of Lake Garda and in the Dolomite Mountains; and along the Isonzo River near where it joins the northern end of the Adriatic Sea. Neither area offered very good terrain for fighting, but while the Isonzo could be seen from the top of barren and jagged hills, the Trentino was worse—fine mountaineering country but no place for military maneuvers.

The Italian chief-of-staff, General Luigi Cadorna, was not a very good general. The difficult terrain did not help, but even so the only plan he could think of was to make his main attack, and keep attacking, in the Isonzo sector, while his specialist mountain troops did what they could in the Trentino. Cadorna planned complicated battles, but took too little account of the difficulties his men actually faced on the ground.

The only part of the Isonzo front that could realistically be used for attacking was about 20 miles (32 km) wide and, whatever Cadorna planned, his attacks ended up battering head-on at the tough Austro-Hungarian positions. There were four battles along the Isonzo following this pattern in 1915. The Italians had about 180,000 casualties to 120,000 Austro-Hungarians and gained almost no ground at all.

Stalemate on the Isonzo

There was much the same story in the Fifth Battle of the Isonzo in March 1916, but after that the Austro-Hungarians began planning an attack of their own. The Austro-Hungarians finally had some spare troops after the defeat of Serbia at the end of 1915. They planned their own major offensive. However, the Austro-Hungarian chief-of-staff, General Conrad von Hötzendorf, was as badly out of touch as Cadorna. He ordered an attack in the Trentino region, but did not even bother to see what the area was like.

The Austro-Hungarians concentrated 160,000 men against 100,000 Italians in this sector and made substantial gains when their attack began on May 14. However, bad weather and the mountainous country meant that they could not keep the pressure up on their enemies. By the end of the month the attack had come to a halt, and soon after that the Austro-Hungarian reserves were called away to fight a Russian offensive on the Eastern Front.

By August 1916 it was back to the brutal series of attacks over the Isonzo. The Sixth Battle of the Isonzo in August was followed by the Seventh in September, the Eighth in October, the Ninth in November, and then the Tenth Battle in May 1917. Despite outnumbering the Austro-Hungarian defenders between

MOUNTAIN WARFARE

Much of the fighting between Italy and Austria-Hungary took place in the mountainous Trentino region. The jagged peaks here are bitterly cold and snow-covered in the winter and often baking hot in the summer. It was hard enough to walk or climb from one place to another without someone shooting at you into the bargain.

It was impossible to dig trenches. Each side tried to capture and hold rocky strongpoints high above enemy positions. The higher up they were, the better you could shoot down on the enemy. However, the higher they were, the colder they were, and the harder it was to bring in vital supplies and evacuate the wounded.

Both sides had to employ specially trained mountain troops in the fighting. These men had to have all the skills of mountaineers simply to move around and survive in such bleak and dangerous locations, and they had to fight as soldiers as well.

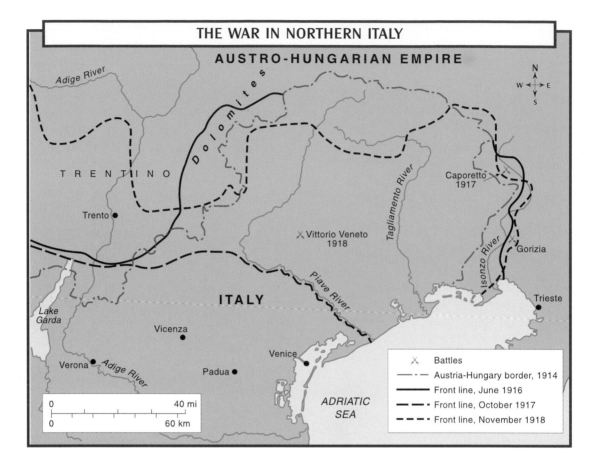

THE WAR IN NORTHERN ITALY

AUSTRO-HUNGARIAN EMPIRE

Adige River

Dolomites

TRENTINO

Trento

Tagliamento River

Caporetto
1917

Vittorio Veneto
1918

Isonzo River

Gorizia

Piave River

ITALY

Lake Garda

Vicenza

Venice

Trieste

Verona · Adige River

Padua

ADRIATIC SEA

✗	Battles
—·—·—	Austria-Hungary border, 1914
———	Front line, June 1916
— — —·	Front line, October 1917
- - - -	Front line, November 1918

0 — 40 mi
0 — 60 km

The Italian campaign was one of the most difficult of the whole war. Both sides fought in mountainous terrain, where the elements were as dangerous as the enemy. Many troops suffered from the intense cold of winter. Their generals had to work hard to keep them supplied even during better weather.

two and three to one, the total Italian advance in the first ten Isonzo battles was only about 12 miles (18 km). Only one attack, the Sixth, which captured the town of Gorizia on the Austro-Hungarian side of the river, could remotely be called successful. In all of these battles some 160,000 Italians had died.

Defeat at Caporetto

Cadorna was not ready to give up. In August 1917, he assembled his strongest attack force yet and launched the Eleventh Battle of the Isonzo. This time the Italians did better, pushing forward six miles (9 km) in one sector. The Austro-Hungarians called for help from their German allies and, when German troops arrived at the front, Cadorna realized it was time to fight defensively.

The Italian forces still slightly outnumbered their enemies, but the German and Austro-Hungarian troops were concentrated in the crucial sectors, trained in new attacking tactics, and equipped with a new type of poison gas. When they attacked on October 24, they smashed the Italian front wide open. This Battle of Caporetto was a disaster for the Italians. They had to retreat over 70 miles (112 km) to the Piave River. The advance only halted when French and British forces arrived to help the Italians.

In June 1918, the Austro-Hungarians attacked once again, but their generals had underestimated how well the Italians had recovered from the Caporetto disaster. Although the Austro-Hungarians made some early progress, Italian resistance increased. A sudden Italian counterattack forced the Austro-Hungarians to fall back. The Austro-Hungarian army was already badly strained by its experiences on the Eastern Front. This failure made these problems worse and added to the pressures that would soon lead to the defeat of the Austro-Hungarian Empire.

Austro-Hungarian collapse

By October 1918, with the Germans and their allies retreating on every other front, the new Italian chief-of-staff, General Armando Diaz, decided that the moment had come for a new Italian offensive.

Assisted by substantial British and French forces, as well as a few U.S. troops who had been sent to aid the Italians after the United States had declared war against the Central Powers on April 6, 1917, the Allies attacked across the Piave River and in the Trentino on October 23, 1918. French and British forces broke through. The Austro-Hungarians quickly collapsed.

Over 300,000 Austro-Hungarians were taken prisoner in this final Allied offensive, known as the Battle of Vittorio Veneto. It was the largest Italian victory of the war and the most decisive. The day after the battle ended, October 28, the Austro-Hungarians asked the Allied powers for an armistice (an end to the fighting), which duly came into effect on November 4.

Two Italian soldiers wearing gas masks on sentry duty in a frontline trench in the Isonzo sector of the Italian front. Deeper trenches, as seen here, offered the best protection.

THE BATTLE FOR MESOPOTAMIA

In 1914 the Ottoman Empire included a province known as Mesopotamia, whose borders were roughly the same as those of the modern country of Iraq. Oil had been found in the region only a few years before World War I. Oil was not as important in 1914 as in the modern world—there were far fewer cars and trucks, and most ships used coal to fuel their engines—but it was still a vital product. Britain's need for oil and its wish to knock Turkey out of the war led to major campaigns being fought in the region.

A gunboat on the Tigris River in Mesopotamia opens fire on a Turkish position during the first British attempt to reach Baghdad in 1915. Despite early successes, the British were decisively defeated at Kut-al-Amara in April 1916.

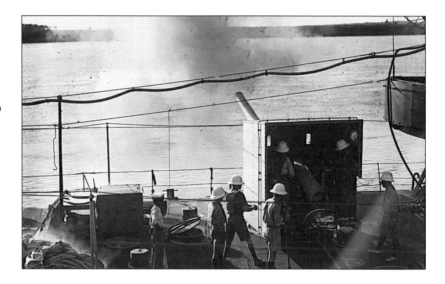

Britain's navy especially needed oil, and in 1913 Britain had made a deal with Persia (an independent country roughly the same as modern Iran) that gave the British access to its biggest oil field. This oil field could easily be attacked from Turkish-controlled Mesopotamia, so when war broke out Britain sent troops to protect it. This was how and why the fighting in this area started.

Russia also had oil interests in the region, around Baku on the Caspian Sea. As British forces began to occupy southern Persia to protect their oil supplies in 1914, the Russians began to move into northern Persia to protect theirs as well.

Britain sent troops from India to the Persian Gulf. These moved against Mesopotamia as soon as war was declared between Britain and the Ottoman Empire on November 5, 1914. The first

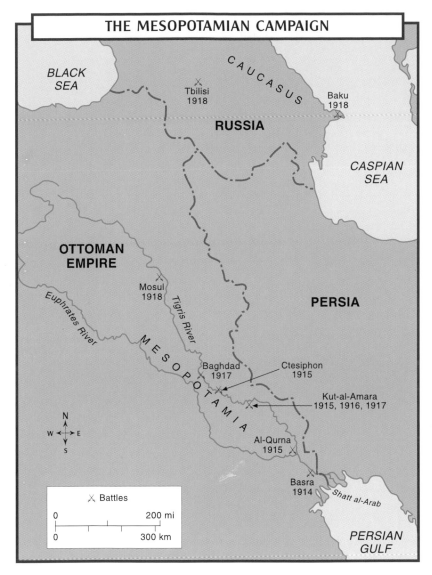

THE MESOPOTAMIAN CAMPAIGN

BLACK SEA

CAUCASUS

Tbilisi 1918

Baku 1918

RUSSIA

CASPIAN SEA

OTTOMAN EMPIRE

Mosul 1918

Tigris River

PERSIA

Euphrates River

MESOPOTAMIA

Baghdad 1917

Ctesiphon 1915

Kut-al-Amara 1915, 1916, 1917

N
W ← → E
S

Al-Qurna 1915

Basra 1914

Shatt al-Arab

✗ Battles

0   200 mi
0   300 km

PERSIAN GULF

The British badly mismanaged the early stages of the war in Mesopotamia. They did not understand the difficulties of fighting in the desert. However, by 1917 they had mastered the art of supply and were able to defeat the Turkish forces opposing them.

objective was to protect the Shatt al-Arab waterway along which oil supplies from Persia reached the Persian Gulf. A British warship bombarded a Turkish fort near the entrance to the Shatt al-Arab on November 6. Riverboats and land forces then captured Basra on November 23. As reinforcements for the initial force had arrived, the British now decided to capture Baghdad, the Mesopotamian capital. Neither the troops nor their commanders realized just how difficult the terrain and weather conditions would make their advance.

British artillery in action during the latter stages of the war in Mesopotamia. By 1918 the British had committed sufficient military resources to the campaign to defeat the Turks.

A British general, Charles Townshend, began an advance up the Tigris River in May 1915. Townshend's men captured Al-Qurna at the end of May and won a battle at Kut-al-Amara in September. The Turks pulled back to Ctesiphon, some 20 miles (32 km) south of Baghdad. Townshend's troops attacked them there between November 22 and 26.

The Turks had about 18,000 troops and Townshend about 11,000. Even so Townshend's attacks nearly broke through on the first day of the battle. The Turks held out and by the fourth day Townshend's army had suffered some 4,000 casualties. Turkish losses were heavier, but the British and Indian troops were exhausted. The British had advanced some 400 miles (640 km) from the sea and were short of supplies. They had to retreat. They fell back to Kut-al-Amara, only to be surrounded there and eventually forced to surrender on April 29, 1916.

Race for the oil fields

By December 1916 the British were ready to advance once again. Their new commander, Sir Frederick Maude, was a far better general than his predecessors, and his forces had been greatly reinforced. Maude's troops beat the Turks under Khalil Pasha in two battles, at Kut-al-Amara in February 1917 and near Baghdad in early March. After these successes the British captured Baghdad itself on March 11.

Maude sensibly halted his forces at this point to avoid the heat of the Mesopotamian summer. The British moved forward a little farther later in the year, but Maude himself died of cholera. With the main objective of Baghdad now secure, the British decided to halt their advance in Mesopotamia for most of 1918.

Following Russia's collapse on the Eastern Front in November 1917 (see pages 54–55), their forces in Persia and the Caucasus region became very weak. The British therefore worried more about keeping the Turks and the Germans away from the oil fields of northern Persia and along the Caspian Sea than about extending their advance in Mesopotamia. The main British effort in the region in the first half of 1918 was therefore the sending of a force under General Lionel Dunsterville from Baghdad north and east into Persia and to Baku on the Caspian.

After the Allied victories in Palestine in September 1918 (see page 23), it was obvious to the British that the Ottoman Empire was about to collapse. In October the British forces in Mesopotamia were ordered to join in the general Allied advance. Once again the objective was a group of oil fields, this time around Mosul in northern Mesopotamia. The Turkish Sixth Army was easily beaten in a few days of fighting and surrendered on October 30, the same day the Turks agreed to a general armistice. The British then pushed on farther to the north and eventually occupied Mosul two weeks later, a victory that marked the end of the fighting. The British had about 80,000 casualties in the course of the entire campaign, including 27,500 dead.

BAKU AND "DUNSTERFORCE"

On January 27, 1918, a British force commanded by General Lionel Dunsterville set out northeastward from Baghdad toward the oil fields of northern Persia and the Russian territories by the Caspian Sea. Russian power in the region had collapsed following the Russian defeats on the Eastern Front in 1917.

Soon the Turks, Germans, and British were in a race to see who could seize the oil fields first. Dunsterville and his men, who were known as "Dunsterforce," reached the southern shores of the Caspian by mid-February but at the same time the Turks were advancing fast through the Caucasus Mountains. The Germans joined in a little later, shipping troops across the Black Sea, who then marched inland to capture Tbilisi in June.

The British advanced farther to occupy Baku in August, only to be forced to retreat after heavy fighting in September. The British reoccupied the town in November, but by then the war was over.

Dunsterville has another claim to fame besides his military exploits. He was a schoolmate of the writer Rudyard Kipling and was the model for the character of Stalky, who appears in one of Kipling's most famous books.

THE FIGHT FOR AFRICA

At the start of World War I almost all of Africa was ruled by one or another of the European countries. Britain and France had the largest colonies, but Germany controlled several others. British naval power ensured that these colonies would be completely cut off from Germany throughout the war. All of them were invaded and eventually captured by Allied forces in the course of the conflict. However, the campaigns in Africa were a huge drain on Allied resources, and the fighting did not end until late in 1918.

Local African troops, known as askaris, attend a parade organized by their German officers. They outfought the Allies throughout World War I, surrendering only after the war in Europe had ended.

The war in Africa involved European soldiers and local troops. Some of the troops who fought on both sides were whites, recruited both from Europe and from the local colonial populations. Most, however, were black Africans plus, on the British side, a large number of men from India. In addition to the combat forces every army employed many thousands of Africans as porters to carry supplies and as laborers.

Togoland (now known as Togo) was the smallest German colony. British and French troops forced the small German forces there to surrender within a month of the start of the war in August 1914. Kamerun (modern Cameroon) held out longer,

PAUL VON LETTOW-VORBECK

Before World War I Colonel Paul von Lettow-Vorbeck had fought with the German army in China and southwest Africa, where Germany had important colonies. He was appointed to command German forces in East Africa at the start of 1914. Lettow-Vorbeck held the Allies off throughout 1914 and 1915, defeating a British seaborne invasion of Tanga in German East Africa (now Tanzania) in November 1914. By 1916, however, the Allies had assembled a far larger force than he could ever hope to defeat.

Lettow-Vorbeck decided his task was to hold out as long as possible and keep the enemy troops occupied in Africa when they might have been better employed in the war in Europe. The enemy troops could only advance slowly against him because there were almost no roads and the terrain and weather were very difficult. Lettow-Vorbeck used hit-and-run tactics to strike suddenly at them and then retreat before his men could be defeated.

His operations took him across much of East Africa, including what are now Kenya, Mozambique, and Zimbabwe. When Lettow-Vorbeck surrendered on November 23, 1918, he still had over 3,000 of his men with him.

Lettow-Vorbeck led Germany's colonial forces in East Africa in World War I.

until March 1916. Eventually over 60,000 British and French troops were used to defeat the 10,000 German and local troops. The British and French lost about 4,000 dead, mostly from disease. German Southwest Africa (modern Namibia) was attacked mainly by troops from the British colony of South Africa. The South Africans quickly captured the few railroad lines in the country and took Windhuk (now Windhoek), the capital, in May 1915. The Germans surrendered soon after.

German East Africa, now mostly part of Tanzania, was the most important of Germany's African colonies and proved to be the hardest to capture. The German commander, Colonel (later General) Paul von Lettow-Vorbeck, proved to be a master of guerrilla warfare. He never had more than 16,000 men, about one quarter of them European, but at one time or another over 130,000 Allied troops were used against him. Yet at the end of the war he was still fighting, and only surrendered because Germany had been defeated in Europe.

THE WAR AT SEA

The war at sea in World War I began with the rival fleets of both Britain and Germany looking for a single decisive victory. There never was such a victory, but the Germans, with a smaller navy, also tried to distract the larger British navy by using small fleets of warships or even single vessels to strike against merchant ships or isolated colonies. However, Britain's key lifeline was across the North Atlantic. Here the Germans used their U-boats (submarines) to wage the first underwater campaign in the history of warfare.

The British-built Dreadnought, a fast, and heavily armed battleship, changed naval warfare. The world's great maritime powers copied the design after its launch in 1906.

For over 100 years before the start of World War I, Britain had easily the world's strongest navy and by far the largest merchant fleet. Maritime trade was vital to Britain's prosperity and to the very survival of the British people—half of Britain's food was imported. However, from the late 1800s on Germany began to build a strong navy and threaten Britain's position.

Without this challenge Britain might have stayed out of World War I, but instead Britain formed an alliance with France and in 1905 began building a fleet of modern dreadnoughts, large,

powerful battleships. When war began the British navy had 29 of these dreadnoughts in service against Germany's 18.

Britain's strategy for the naval war was based on the idea of blockade. This had three objectives. First, to protect Britain's trade, mainly by keeping Germany's warships imprisoned in their home ports; second, to stop all trade by Germany's own merchant ships; and third, to protect Britain's overseas trade.

One of these objectives proved easy to accomplish. Within days of the start of the war virtually all of Germany's merchant ships had either been captured by the British or had taken refuge in neutral ports. However, the other objectives caused greater problems for the British.

The rival fleets clash

The Germans gave their main forces the title of the High Seas Fleet, but this name proved to be a false boast. Besides having the larger fleet, Britain's geographical position effectively blocked German access to the oceans. Only narrow channels led out of the North Sea to the Atlantic Ocean, and these were guarded by Britain's naval forces or protected by minefields. To reach the high seas, Germany would have had to defeat the British navy's Grand Fleet first.

Britain's lead over Germany in numbers of major ships seemed comfortable enough to rule this possibility out, but it was far from being true. For a time in 1915, for example, with some ships under repair and because of other problems, Britain's Grand Fleet had only one battleship more than the Germans—not nearly enough margin for safety.

If the British navy were defeated, Britain would lose the war. This placed a huge responsibility on the Grand Fleet's commander, Admiral John Jellicoe, to make no mistakes in his battle tactics. A British politician said that Jellicoe was "the only man on either side who could lose the war in an afternoon."

THE DREADNOUGHT

Dreadnought was the name of a British battleship launched in 1906, which was the first of a new kind of warship that became known as the "dreadnought battleship." Throughout the second half of the 19th century, navies had used bigger and bigger long-range guns and thicker armor on their ships, but had never worked out an ideal way to combine these features in one vessel. *Dreadnought* changed all that.

The top navies rushed to build dreadnought fleets and gain superiority over their rivals. In the lead-up to World War I Britain's navy built the most dreadnoughts and remained the strongest fleet in the world. But the British were very worried by the increasingly powerful German dreadnought fleet.

During World War I Britain's battleships kept the upper hand over their German rivals, but by the end of the war two new naval powers, the United States and Japan, were competing for world naval supremacy.

The remains of a British warship, the Invincible, *pictured shortly after the Battle of Jutland. Most of the crew of the* Invincible *went down with the ship. Only six men were saved by the destroyer* Badger *(seen here on the right).*

The German naval leaders were very cautious, and there was only one large battle between the two rival fleets in the whole of the war. This battle was fought on the afternoon and into the night of May 31, 1916, and is called the Battle of Jutland by the British and the Battle of the Skagerrak by the Germans. The fighting took place in the North Sea, about 50 miles (80 km) off the coast of Denmark.

The Germans came off best in the early stages of the battle, but the British, with 37 dreadnoughts against 21, soon gained the upper hand. Jellicoe almost trapped the Germans and the German commander, Admiral Reinhard Scheer, had to turn and flee. By then it was a dull hazy evening, with visibility made worse by the smoke from the guns and funnels of the 250 ships involved in the battle. The Germans slipped away into the gloom and escaped before the next morning.

After Jutland the British blockade remained as effective as before, while the German High Seas Fleet remained in port for the rest of the war, contributing nothing whatsoever to the German war effort.

Submarine warfare

If Germany's fleet of surface warships failed to accomplish much, its U-boats were a different matter. World War I was the first conflict in which submarines were employed. The first really practicable submarines had only been invented in the 1890s, and their development up to 1914 was very slow. Navies had not really learned how to use them, or how to defend against them, or how they fitted in with the international laws of war.

Throughout the war both sides' submarines took every chance they could to sink warships, but in February 1915 Germany also decided to use U-boats to impose its own blockade, sinking British and neutral merchant ships carrying cargoes to and from Britain. This first period of submarine attacks lasted until September 1915, when the Germans stopped attacks because of protests from the United States and other neutral countries.

American protests

These protests were made because many American citizens were killed when ships were sunk. This was especially the case on May 7, 1915, when the German submarine U-20 sank the passenger liner *Lusitania*, killing 1,198 people, including 128 Americans. The Germans renewed their all-out attacks for a brief period in 1916 but again stopped them after American protests.

At the start of 1917 the Germans decided that the danger of drawing the United States into the war was a risk they had to take. They thought that they could sink enough ships to starve Britain into surrendering. Even if this meant that America declared war, Germany believed the war would be over before America was ready to fight effectively on the Allied side.

The strategy nearly worked. The U-boats sank over 1,000 British ships in 1917. By May the British government calculated that there was only six weeks' supply of food in the whole country—and the British admirals had no idea how to stop the U-boat attacks. As a last resort they tried introducing a convoy system (merchant ships traveling together with warships), and found that their losses declined.

British shipping losses in 1918 were less than half of those in 1917, so in the end the U-boat campaign failed. Even worse for the Germans, it was the main reason why the United States declared war on them in April 1917. In addition to failing in their war against British trade and food supplies, the U-boats also failed to halt the transportation of U.S. troops across the Atlantic to France in 1917–18.

The liner Lusitania *slides beneath the waves after being struck by a torpedo fired by the German submarine U-20 on May 7, 1915. Among the dead were more than 100 U.S. citizens.*

THE STRUGGLE AT VERDUN

By 1916 it had become obvious that there were no quick victories to be won by either side on the Western Front. The German generals had kept their forces on the defensive in France and Belgium throughout 1915 while they concentrated on defeating Russia. For 1916, however, their chief-of-staff, General Erich von Falkenhayn, persuaded the German emperor, Wilhelm II, to attack France in massive strength. The objective chosen was the heavily defended town of Verdun, close to France's frontier with Germany.

German troops pictured shortly before heading for their frontline trenches at Verdun. Some carry extra ammunition.

The attack Falkenhayn planned was designed, he said, "to bleed the French army to death." He wanted to kill France's soldiers but did not think it was especially important to capture large areas of French territory. His idea was to win the war by a process of attrition, wearing the enemy resistance down to a point where the French would have to surrender.

For hundreds of years before World War I the town of Verdun, about 120 miles (192 km) east of Paris, had been one of the major strongpoints protecting France's border region with Germany. Falkenhayn guessed correctly that the French would commit everything they had to hold Verdun if he attacked in strength. He intended to use his powerful artillery to ensure that French casualties became unbearably high. However, Falkenhayn never clearly explained how he expected to do this without causing massive German casualties at the same time.

A slogging match

The German attack began on February 21, 1916, on an eight-mile (13-km) front to the north of Verdun. Verdun was protected by a ring of fortresses on a line of low hills overlooking the town. By 1916 many of the fortresses' heavy cannon had been taken away for use in offensives elsewhere on the Western Front. Although their defenses were run down, the fortresses would play a key role in the battle to come. In the first few days of the battle most of the troops originally defending the French front line were wiped out. The Germans captured Fort Douaumont, one of the strongest in the defense line, on February 25, and their newspapers told the world they had achieved a great victory.

In fact, a turning point had arrived. The French high command decided that they could hold Verdun. More and more French reinforcements were arriving, and a new commander, General Henri-Philippe Pétain, was appointed to lead the defense. Pétain quickly reorganized the French forces and they started to use their artillery effectively against the Germans.

Even so the Germans extended their offensive with new attacks north of the town in early March. These were concentrated around a hill called Mort Homme, a name that means

---

LA VOIE SACRÉE

"La Voie Sacrée" is French for "the Sacred Way" and was the name given in 1916 to the main supply route for the French armies fighting at Verdun. In 1916, the town of Verdun was joined to the rest of France by one railroad line, which was cut by German shelling at the start of the battle.

The only alternative was a single minor road into the town from the south. Thousands of trucks were brought from all over France to bring supplies and reinforcements into the battle along this one road. Thousands of soldiers worked frantically to repair the road in the brief gaps between the supply convoys.

Three-quarters of the soldiers in the French army fought at Verdun at some stage in the battle, some of them having several periods of frontline service. Every soldier rode into battle along the Sacred Way and knew that he faced a dreadful ordeal. Many of those Frenchmen who traveled down that minor but vital supply road to Verdun never returned.

"dead man" in French and proved to be horribly appropriate. The battlefield turned into a scene of slaughter. Neither side was prepared to give up an inch of territory, so attacks and bombardments were instantly met by fierce counterattacks and yet more shelling. Thousands on each side died, but gradually the German front line crept forward.

Attack after attack

Pétain was promoted to command a larger part of the French army on May 1, and a new leader, General Robert Nivelle, took over the running of the Verdun battle. Nivelle's first counterattacks failed, and by early June the Germans were pushing forward again. They captured another important defensive strongpoint, Fort Vaux, on June 7.

HENRI-PHILIPPE PÉTAIN

Marshal Henri-Philippe Pétain was one of France's greatest heroes during World War I, but was condemned to death for betraying his country in World War II. Pétain was not one of France's top soldiers at the start of World War I. One of the reasons he had not been promoted was that he did not believe in the attacking tactics that most French generals of the time favored. After the war started, he proved to be so good at his job that he quickly moved up the ranks until he took command at Verdun in 1916.

A large number of French troops mutinied in 1917, because of their poor treatment and huge casualties. They refused to attack, although willing to defend their positions if attacked. When Pétain was made chief-of-staff he made sure that the soldiers got better food and medical care. He also stopped all reckless attacks. These measures ended the mutinies and ensured that the French would be able to fight on into 1918.

During World War II, when France was occupied by Nazi Germany, Pétain led the French government that cooperated with the Nazis. After the war he was tried as a traitor, but said he had only been trying to protect the French people. Pétain was convicted and sentenced to death. The sentence was not carried out, and he died in prison.

On June 22 the Germans attacked again, this time using a new type of poison gas that the French gas masks did not protect against. Verdun seemed certain to fall. Pétain—or possibly Nivelle—issued special orders the next day, which included a phrase that would become France's most famous slogan of the war, "Ils ne passeront pas!"—"They shall not pass!" Somehow the French held on.

So far the French army had borne the brunt of the fighting on the Western Front as a whole, and at Verdun in particular, but now the British were ready to take over as the principal army on the Allied side. Their attack on the Somme River sector began on July 1, and soon the Germans had to withdraw troops from Verdun to reinforce their defenses there.

This did not mean that the fighting at Verdun was over. Vicious attacks and counterattacks from both sides continued through the summer and into the fall. The French objective was to regain the lost territory, but for the Germans it was now clearly a pointless battle they were not going to win. Falkenhayn's strategy was not working, and at the end of August the emperor fired him. The successful command team from the Eastern Front,

The Ravine of the Dead, a painting that captures the horrors of the fighting around Verdun in 1916. Hastily buried corpses were often exposed again by the explosion of artillery shells.

The Germans began the battle for Verdun believing that they could smash the French army. In reality the attacking German troops suffered as much as the French, and the battle ended in December 1916 with neither side having won any advantage.

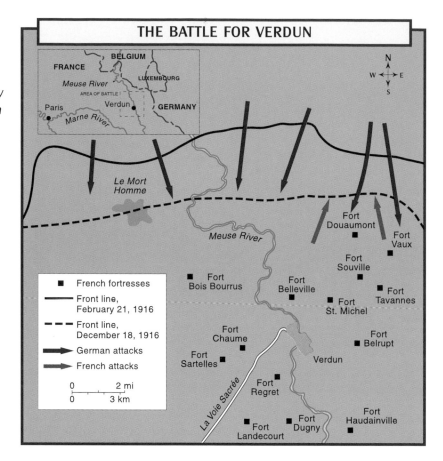

Field Marshal Paul von Hindenburg and General Erich Ludendorff, took over the German army. Hindenburg and Ludendorff immediately stopped all German attacks at Verdun. Both realized that the plan to destroy the French army had little chance of success and that their own losses were so heavy that they threatened the fighting spirit of the German army.

However, the French were not finished yet and decided to counterattack the German forces around Verdun. Nivelle planned a massive offensive for October. The French had built up their artillery strength and devised new tactics to make their bombardment more effective.

The French attacks were successful. They recaptured Fort Douaumont on October 24, the first day of their attack, and soon regained much of the ground that had been lost in the previous eight months of vicious combat. Fort Vaux was recaptured by the French on November 2. More French attacks followed. These continued into the bitter winter weather of December until the battle was finally halted on the 18th. In the last three days of fighting the French captured nearly 120,000 Germans.

About one million men had been killed or wounded in the battle, just over half of them on the French side. Yet little had been achieved apart from the total devastation of the battle area. Both sides were virtually back where they had started out by the close of the fighting. Falkenhayn had begun the assault on Verdun hoping to smash the French army, but by December both armies had in fact suffered equally horribly. Neither side won the Battle of Verdun.

New plans for 1917

Both sides would need different plans for 1917. By the end of the Verdun battle, Hindenburg and Ludendorff were already devising effective new fighting ideas for the German army that seemed to offer a hope of victory. The French army, too, had a new supreme commander for the coming year. General Joseph Joffre was fired in December 1916 and was replaced by Nivelle, who claimed that he could attack as successfully with the whole of the French army as he had in the last weeks at Verdun. Events in 1917 would show that he could not live up to this boast.

French troops man trenches amid the unrecognizable remains of Verdun's Fort Douaumont at the end of the battle in December 1916.

SLAUGHTER ON THE SOMME

The Battle of the Somme in 1916 was the first major battle of the war in which the British forces played the leading role on the Allied side. Britain's small prewar army had been expanded by a massive recruiting campaign, but the new troops and their leaders still had little experience of battle. Canadian, Australian, South African, and New Zealand troops fought alongside the British and had similar problems. The Somme became the grave of many of these enthusiastic recruits but laid the foundations for a skilled army.

A column of earth is thrown into the air after the detonation of tons of explosives placed in a mine under the German trenches. The Somme attack began moments later.

When the Allied generals first planned the Somme battle at the end of 1915, they thought it should be a joint British and French attack. However, because of the pressure the French were under at Verdun, the British part in the Somme battle became much larger. The Somme River region was chosen for the attack because it happened to be where the sectors manned by the British and French troops joined up, not because it was a good place to attack. The Germans held strong defensive positions on high ground overlooking the Allied lines.

THE BRITISH BARRAGE

Before the attack at the Somme began, British artillery fired a preliminary bombardment that lasted for eight days. About 1.7 million shells were fired by 1,400 guns. It was no wonder that the British generals believed that the German front line would be smashed and most of the German troops there killed.

The events of July 1 proved that the British generals were very wrong. The German soldiers spent the week deep underground in their dugouts (bombproof shelters), ready to carry their machine guns up into their trenches at the first sign of the British infantry attack. It was a dreadful experience to be in a dugout under the horrendous noise of an artillery bombardment, never knowing if a direct hit from a big shell would suddenly rip you apart or bury you forever, but it was an experience that many of the defending troops survived.

Too few of the British shells were the high-explosive type that were the only ones effective against enemy fortifications or able to cut through the thick rows of barbed wire that protected the German trenches. The few shells and guns that could do these jobs were distributed too thinly along the 25-mile (40-km) Somme front to have much impact. Almost 20,000 British soldiers died on July 1 mainly because their generals did not understand that at the time.

Every major battle of World War I required a huge amount of planning and preliminary work. Gun positions, field hospitals, ammunition dumps, new trenches, and many other facilities all had to be built, along with a network of new roads and railroads to feed men, ammunition, food, and other supplies into the battle when it began. This could take months especially when, as with the British in 1916, the attacking army had never carried out an operation on such a scale. The key to the British plans, which were developed by General Douglas Haig, was a huge force of artillery guns and shells for the opening bombardment. The bombardment started on June 24 but July 1, when the infantry advance began, is usually described as the first day of the battle.

Artillery was the most important weapon not just of the Somme battle but of the whole war. The British commanders had been hampered by shell shortages in 1915 but thought that at last they had enough supplies for a decisive barrage. They were wrong. More than one quarter of the shells used did not even explode, and most of those that did go off were small shrapnel-type shells. These were effective against enemy troops moving

around in the open, but poor at blasting gaps in barbed wire and useless for smashing defensive positions, the two tasks that were needed.

The British generals thought that the best way to follow up their artillery bombardment was with a slow and steady infantry attack. Lines of troops would march across no-man's-land (the wasteland between the rival lines of trenches) toward the wrecked German front line carrying all the ammunition and supplies they would need for the next few days of fighting deep in German territory.

Disaster on day one

The result was a massacre. The German front lines had not been wrecked at all. As the British troops climbed out of their trenches and began their advance, they were mowed down in the hundreds, many before they had gone more than a few yards. No-man's-land was about 500 yards (450 m) wide on average and some of the attackers got most of the way across only to find that the German barbed wire had not been blasted away by the artillery bombardment. As they struggled to find a way through, hundreds more were cut down by machine guns and artillery.

One of the 40,000 British soldiers wounded on the first day of the Battle of the Somme, July 1, 1916, receives medical attention in a frontline trench near the village of Beaumont Hamel.

Almost 20,000 British soldiers died on July 1, 1916, and another 40,000 were wounded. It was a disastrous day for the British army, the worst in its history. Yet even after this terrible start the British generals kept planning new attacks. The British commanders had aimed to break through the German defenses completely at the start of the battle. They still hoped to achieve such a breakthrough in the later stages of the fighting, but by then their real objective was a more limited one of gradually wearing the German strength down and paving the way for a future decisive victory.

It might have seemed better to have called off the battle, rather than change to this strategy of attrition, but this was impossible. How could the British have stopped attacking after one day, however bad it had been, when the French desperately needed help after more than four months of fighting at Verdun? Even if the British had scaled down their offensive, there were still the Germans to think of. Their generals always counter-attacked to try to recapture any ground that the British had taken. In the four months of the Somme battle the Germans made well over 300 attacks of various sizes.

Two of the British attacks in the later stages were particularly important, the ones on July 14 and September 15. The advance almost broke through the German lines on July 14, but the British reserves arrived too slowly to grab the opportunity. Throughout the war many such chances were missed by both

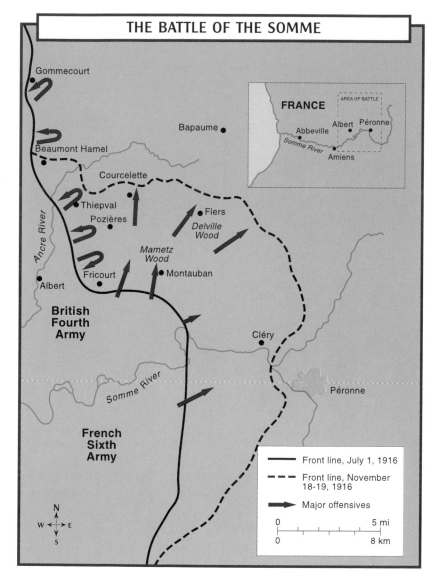

THE BATTLE OF THE SOMME

Gommecourt

Bapaume

FRANCE

AREA OF BATTLE

Abbeville · Albert Péronne

Somme River

Amiens

Beaumont Hamel

Courcelette

Thiepval
Pozières
Flers
Delville Wood

Mametz Wood

Fricourt · Montauban

Albert

British Fourth Army

Cléry

Somme River

Péronne

French Sixth Army

Front line, July 1, 1916

Front line, November 18-19, 1916

Major offensives

| 0 | | | | 5 mi |
| 0 | | | | 8 km |

N
W E
S

The Battle of the Somme lasted from July to November 1916. It was the first large-scale British attack on the Western Front, and it began badly. However, the British continued the battle. When it ended, the British had advanced less than 10 miles (16 km) and suffered over 400,000 casualties.

British troops and a Mark I tank pictured near the village of Flers, which was captured on September 17. Note the field telephone operator lying on the tank's right track. Poor communications equipment hampered the British control of the fighting in the Somme offensive.

sides. Since portable radios did not exist there was no quick way for advancing troops to send messages to their generals or reserve forces. It took hours to carry out new orders or maneuvers, and the defenders would use that time to rebuild their positions.

Ending the battle

On September 15, 1916, the British used a new secret weapon, the tank, for the first time ever in war. The tanks of 1916 were clumsy and unreliable. Only 11 out of the 47 the British had available actually did any fighting—most of the rest broke down. A few German troops were panicked by the strange metal monsters and the British captured some ground, but by the end of the day hardly any of the tanks were still in running order. The tank had a long way to go before it became an effective weapon of war.

FIELD MARSHAL SIR DOUGLAS HAIG

Field Marshal Sir Douglas Haig was the commander-in-chief of the British troops fighting on the Western Front from December 1915 to the end of the war. He planned and commanded the major British offensives at the Somme in 1916 and others until the end of the war.

Haig was a career soldier who had seen service in northern and southern Africa at the end of the 19th century. At the beginning of World War I, Haig commanded the British First Corps and fought in all the major battles on the Western Front in 1914. Haig was promoted to command all the British forces in France after his predecessor, Sir John French, was fired in December 1915.

Haig masterminded the Somme offensive in 1916 and was promoted to field marshal, despite the attack's failure. Some historians believe Haig was a poor commander, but he was a great organizer of the British forces in France, was open to new ideas, such as the tank, and had a good working relationship with his French allies, unlike some British generals.

By the end of the battle, around November 18, the British had advanced no more than six miles (10 km) from their original front line. Almost 100,000 British Empire troops had died in the process, along with 50,000 Frenchmen. No one knows how many Germans were killed: estimates range from about 100,000 to 160,000. For every man killed on each side, roughly another three were wounded.

No matter what the exact casualty count may have been, neither side really won the Battle of the Somme. The battle had been a truly horrible experience for all who fought there and the morale, that is to say the enthusiasm and will to win, of all the armies had been badly damaged. However, the British soldiers and their leaders had learned many lessons. The inexperienced troops of July had become battle-hardened. Their generals thought this was a good basis for more attacks in 1917.

Up to the end of 1916 the German army fought more skillfully than any of its opponents, but many of its best officers and sergeants had been killed by then. Ludendorff worried that the German army would lose its superiority. If there were more battles like the Somme, he thought the German lead would disappear completely. Ludendorff knew that the Allies would keep attacking on the Western Front and accordingly planned a new strategy for 1917.

WAR IN THE AIR

World War I was the first conflict in which air power played an important part. Hot-air balloons had featured occasionally in 19th century wars, and their more modern equivalent, the lighter-than-air airship, remained important in 1914, but the real developments were in heavier-than-air airplanes. These were used in limited number in 1914, but by the final year of the war, aircraft were playing an important role in supporting ground operations and were also carrying out long-range bombing missions.

France's Aéronautique Militaire was probably the most powerful and efficient air force in the world with about 130 front-line aircraft at the start of the war. By 1918, air power had become a vital component of every battle plan by land or sea and, by way of comparison, at the end of the war the largest air force in the world was Britain's Royal Air Force, with over 22,000 planes. Although aircraft played a part in every theater of the war, both sides sent by far their strongest air forces to the Western Front. The air battle over the trenches soon became as fierce and deadly as the fighting on the ground.

Reconnaissance missions

The aircraft used by all sides in 1914 were flimsy and underpowered. They carried no weapons at all, either for use against other aircraft or to attack enemy forces on the ground. The only military role that they were expected to do was that of reconnaissance—surveying enemy territory and

A British fighter pilot, Lieutenant Warneford, shoots down a German Zeppelin airship over southern England. Airships were gradually replaced by long-range bombers.

activity. Even in this role their capabilities were limited. Pilots had no means of signaling the information they discovered to friendly troops unless they flew back to their own territory to drop a message or landed and delivered one personally.

The Farman MF-7, also known as the Longhorn Farman and used by France and Britain, was typical of the aircraft available in 1914. It was an unarmed "pusher" biplane (with the engine and propeller mounted behind the fuselage) with a top speed of about 60 mph (96 km/h). By comparison, the 1918 Spad S-XIII fighter, used by France and the United States, was twice as fast and carried two machine guns as armament. At the end of the war Britain was introducing the Handley Page V-1500 bomber, capable of carrying a large load of bombs deep into Germany itself.

New aircraft and new roles

By the end of the war it was not only the aircraft that had changed beyond recognition but also the range of tasks they performed. Reconnaissance remained the most important air role throughout the war, but the reconnaissance planes were soon joined by fighters and bombers.

Within a few months of the war's start, the capabilities of reconnaissance aircraft were transformed by the introduction of aerial photography. Especially when the front lines changed little during the long periods of trench warfare, aerial photographs were used to build up extremely detailed maps of enemy positions.

Another reconnaissance mission was artillery spotting, that is observing where artillery shells were actually landing and signaling to the gunners to correct their aim. At first reconnaissance aircraft tried using flags and colored flares to signal with, but radios were gradually introduced. For both types of missions the

STRATEGIC BOMBING

Most aerial bombing in World War I was carried out against enemy army positions and installations at or near the front lines, but by 1918 there had also been many aircraft attacks on targets far from the front. Such raids, aimed at targets such as munitions factories or transportation centers, were the first examples of what is now known as strategic bombing.

A German airplane dropped bombs on Paris during the first month of the war. The first long-range raid by the Allies was carried out by the British later in 1914, with its target being the factory where Germany's Zeppelin airships were made.

German Zeppelins carried out strategic bombing raids up to 1917, when they were replaced by Gotha aircraft. The Gothas and the British equivalents, the Handley Page 0/100 and 0/400, which were also used in 1917 and 1918, proved to be very vulnerable to the enemy fighters and anti-aircraft defenses they met.

Air raids caused little physical damage and relatively few casualties, but they were a terrifying reminder that the war could reach and hurt everyone, not just the soldiers at the front.

Members of a German squadron arm a Gotha long-range bomber prior to a raid on southern England, August 1918.

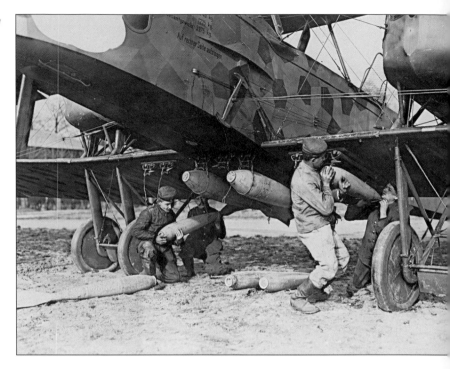

reconnaissance planes had to fly over a particular area on a straight and level course. This made them vulnerable to attack from the fighter planes that both sides quickly developed.

Air warfare weapons

Bombers, too, quickly came into action. It did not take long for grenades dropped by hand by a crewman to be replaced by larger bombs carried on a bomb rack. By 1918, bombers included very large two- and four-engined types designed for long-range strategic bombing against the enemy homeland and smaller designs for use over the battlefield. Some even carried armor plating to protect their pilots and crucial components from the danger of enemy fire during low-level missions.

At first some pilots used pistols and other handheld weapons to try to shoot their enemies down, but it was obvious that machine guns were much more effective. The easiest way to use a machine gun for air combat was to mount it in front of the pilot and for him to aim his gun by flying straight at the enemy. Rear- or sideways-firing machine guns operated by a second crewman were soon fitted into many aircraft also, but these were only effective for defense.

Front-mounted machine guns worked well for "pusher" type aircraft, but designers soon discovered that these had a limited performance. "Tractor" type aircraft, that is with the engine and propeller at the front, could usually fly faster and higher, which was an obvious advantage for a fighter, but the problem was that a machine gun mounted in front of the pilot would shoot his own propeller off before he ever damaged his enemy.

The problem was solved by a Dutch designer, Anton Fokker, who worked for the Germans. He designed a synchronizing device, also known as an interrupter gear, which stopped the machine gun from firing for the instant that one of the propeller blades was in front of the muzzle. This device was first used in the summer of 1915 and gave the Germans complete air superiority until the spring of 1916, by which time the Allies had devised their own versions of it.

The first fighter aces

For the rest of the war first one side then the other held the upper hand on the Western Front, as new aircraft designs came into service and briefly held the advantage over the enemy in armament, speed, maneuverability, or rate of climb. The Germans had two periods when they were on top in this way: from the summer of 1915 into the spring of 1916 and from the fall of 1916 through the spring of 1917. The odds were more even at most other times in the war, apart from the last few months of 1918 by which time the Allies had built up a huge superiority.

The best pilots became famous as air aces. Newspapers and government propaganda sources boasted of their exploits and described them as modern-day knights, jousting chivalrously with their enemies above the clouds. Pilots like Eddie Rickenbacker, the top American ace with 26 "kills," and Canada's Billy Bishop with 72 aircraft shot down, became household names. However, even for the top aces the prospects of survival were at least as grim as for the ordinary soldier in the trenches. Germany's top ace, Baron Manfred von Richthofen, the "Red Baron," shot down at least 80 enemy aircraft, more than any other pilot, but even he was killed in 1918.

Top German air ace Baron Manfred von Richthofen (left) leads other fighters from his squadron during a mission over the Western Front.

COLLAPSE IN THE EAST

By 1916 Russia's industries were at last beginning to supply its armies with the guns and other materials they needed. Russia's generals, too, were commanding their men more efficiently. The huge casualties of the first two years of war and the many upheavals in life at home in Russia were soon to have a decisive impact on the war on the Eastern Front, however. Soldiers became unwilling to fight and disobeyed orders. The Russian army began to fall apart, which allowed Germany to send troops to the Western Front.

Russian revolutionary Lenin addresses a crowd outside a railroad station in Petrograd (now St. Petersburg), April 1917.

During 1916, however, this threat had not yet become clear. The Brusilov Offensive, an attack against Austria-Hungary, from June to October was Russia's most successful of the war, despite a huge casualty toll. General Aleksei Brusilov's success even persuaded a previously neutral country, Romania, to join the war on the Allied side. However, what happened next showed that the "success" of the Brusilov Offensive was really an illusion.

By virtually knocking the Austro-Hungarian army out of the war, the Russians ensured that Germany would take complete control of the war against them. One of Germany's major war aims was to dominate the whole of Eastern Europe and exploit the whole region economically for Germany's benefit. Romania was the first country to experience just what this ruthless policy meant.

Romania joined the war hoping to grab land from Austria-Hungary. It was a foolish decision. In a three-week campaign in November and December 1916, the Germans overran almost the whole of Romania. For the rest of the war, grain and oil seized from Romania would help feed and fuel the German war effort.

Chaos in Russia

In March 1917 food shortages and other problems brought on a violent upheaval in Russia. Revolution broke out and the czar abdicated (gave up) his throne. A Provisional Government took over and promised the other Allies that Russia would continue to fight. In July 1917 they even organized a new offensive against the Germans, but it soon failed.

Other political groups in Russia had different plans. The Bolshevik party had a radical socialist program to transform Russia, sweeping away those in power and giving ordinary people a much greater political voice, and the effective Bolshevik leaders, Lenin (V.I. Ulyanov) and Leon Trotsky, soon successfully extended their party's power and influence. In November 1917 they took action, seizing power in another revolution.

These events are rather confusingly known as the October Revolution. Russia used a different calendar from the rest of the world in 1917, and the Russian name for the revolution, based on its date in Russia, has become generally accepted. The earlier revolution in March 1917 is known as the February Revolution.

For Russia this was the start of a process that would lead through a bloody civil war to the eventual establishment of the Soviet Union, but in November 1917 Russia was still at war with Germany. In December the Bolshevik leaders began negotiations with the Germans for peace. They agreed to an armistice, that is to say a cease-fire while negotiations proceeded, on the 15th.

A harsh peace treaty

Over the next two months of talks Germany demanded huge tracts of territory, which the Bolsheviks were reluctant to concede. The Germans decided to force the issue and sent their troops advancing deep into Russia. The Bolsheviks had to give in. By the Treaty of Brest-Litovsk, agreed on in March 1918, Germany took control of over 25 percent of the Russian people, 75 percent of Russia's coal and iron resources, and a vast territory covering what are now the independent countries of Estonia, Latvia, Lithuania, Belarus, and the Ukraine.

German forces moved into all these areas to begin the process of ruling and exploiting them for Germany's benefit. With the end of fighting against Russia, many of the German troops, until now committed to the Eastern Front, were redeployed to France, where Germany's leaders planned new offensives for 1918. The outcome of these battles, some of the largest seen in the whole war, would also determine whether Germany would be able to defeat the Allies in the west and keep its new empire in Eastern Europe. The offensive was to be Germany's last gamble.

STALEMATE IN THE WEST

Both sides began 1917 with new plans for their armies on the Western Front. After his successes in the final stages of the Battle of Verdun, General Robert Nivelle was promoted to command the whole French army. Nivelle claimed that he knew the secret of military success, and the French government believed him. He planned a major offensive for the spring. Nivelle believed he could win a crushing victory against the Germans—as did the British, who were also planning to attack the Germans in 1917.

French troops advance during the opening phase of the offensive planned by the overconfident General Robert Nivelle. Nivelle expected to smash through the German front line in a matter of days, but his optimistic plan was quickly abandoned.

The terrible casualties the German army had suffered during the Battle of the Somme and at Verdun in 1916 also made Ludendorff decide on a new strategy for 1917. Battles of attrition, simply exhausting the enemy, Ludendorff decided, would in the long run benefit the Allies because they had more men and other military resources.

Ludendorff ordered that the German army should drop its old policy of automatically counterattacking every Allied advance. He even voluntarily retreated from a large area of captured French territory to a new defensive system, known to the Allies as the Hindenburg Line. He knew that the French and British would keep attacking, and Ludendorff planned to defeat them there.

THE HINDENBURG LINE

German generals were so horrified by their army's huge numbers of casualties in the battles of 1916 that they started work in the fall of 1916 on a vast complex of defensive positions all along the Western Front some 20 or more miles (32 km) behind their existing front lines.

The Germans began to withdraw to their new positions in February 1917 and had completed their move by April. The Allies called the positions the Hindenburg Line (see map, page 62). World War I would be decided on whether or not the British and French, with American support, could break through the Hindenburg Line.

The Hindenburg Line was based on the idea of defense in depth, and the fortified area could be anything up to 12 miles (20 km) deep, with line after line of trenches, strongpoints, and barbed wire backed by artillery support.

During 1916 the Allies had developed the artillery power to smash a traditional trench line. The new system meant that they now faced a network of supporting strongpoints, artillery, and machine-gun positions that could break up any attack. The fighting in 1917 and during the offensives in late 1918 showed just how tough such defenses could be.

The German retreat to the Hindenburg Line meant that Nivelle had to change his plans—the Germans had voluntarily given up some of the territory that Nivelle had planned to capture. Nivelle still said he could break through and win the war. Unfortunately for his men the Germans soon had a very good idea of what Nivelle planned and prepared their defenses.

The French army mutinies

Nivelle's attack, officially known as the Second Battle of the Aisne (the first had taken place in 1914), began on April 16. It was soon obvious that it was not going to result in a decisive victory. Within four days the French had scaled down their efforts after suffering about 120,000 casualties. Limited attacks continued into the second week of May, but with nothing like the decisive results that Nivelle had promised.

By the standards of some earlier battles the results were not all that bad, but the French soldiers had had enough. In addition to horrible casualties, they had also had to put up with awful food, almost no leave, and poor medical services. Starting on about April 29 thousands mutinied, refusing to make any more attacks on the Germans or to obey any other orders from their officers.

The Battle of Passchendaele in Belgium was the British army's major offensive in 1917. Because of bad weather and strong German resistance it was a slogging match. The battle lasted from July until November and the British suffered around 300,000 casualties.

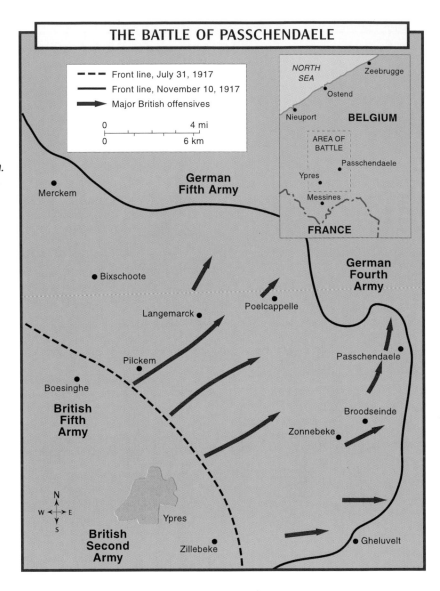

THE BATTLE OF PASSCHENDAELE

- – – Front line, July 31, 1917
- —— Front line, November 10, 1917
- → Major British offensives

0   4 mi
0   6 km

NORTH SEA   Zeebrugge
Ostend
Nieuport   **BELGIUM**
AREA OF BATTLE
Passchendaele
Ypres
Messines
FRANCE

German Fifth Army

Merckem

Bixschoote

Langemarck

Poelcappelle

German Fourth Army

Pilckem

Passchendaele

Boesinghe

British Fifth Army

Broodseinde

Zonnebeke

Ypres

British Second Army

Zillebeke

Gheluvelt

Nivelle was fired from his command on May 15, and Marshal Henri Pétain replaced him. Pétain treated his soldiers well and the mutinies ended, but it would take months for the French army to recover. Well into the summer of 1917, the army was very weak and might have collapsed if the Germans had attacked.

Field Marshal Douglas Haig and the other British generals had never really liked Nivelle's plan, even though they had agreed to support it with an advance of their own in April. Haig had always wanted to attack at the north end of the Western Front around

Ypres. The first stage of the offensive was a clear-cut success for the British. On June 6, they attacked an important German position south of Ypres at Messines. Over the previous months the British had dug 19 mines under the German front lines and filled them with huge amounts of explosives. At zero hour, shortly before the attack, they were detonated and blasted a series of huge gaps in the German lines.

The main British attack began in July and is called the Third Battle of Ypres, or the Battle of Passchendaele. After a long preliminary bombardment the infantry advance started on July 31. The Germans held a strong position made even tougher by concrete pillboxes—small, low structures for machine guns.

Although the British had more artillery and air superiority, the ground conditions and the weather favored the defense. When the battle began so did the torrential rain, while at the same time artillery shells smashed the land drainage system to pieces. The result was that the battlefield became a swamp. The British kept on attacking until the middle of November. By then they had about 300,000 casualties and won five miles (8 km) of ground.

Massed tank attack

Even after all this there was one more major battle to come on the Western Front in 1917. The Battle of Cambrai, (see map page 62) which began on November 20, is known as the world's first tank-led battle. Some 320 British tanks smashed a gap in the German lines but over half of them broke down or were destroyed on the first day. The British did not have reserves available to push forward. German counterattacks pushed the British back.

The year 1917 therefore ended with all the armies on the Western Front having suffered horrendous casualties with little apparent gain. The Allies, however, were awaiting the arrival of reinforcements from the United States, which had declared war the previous April. War had been declared because of attacks on neutral U.S. ships by German submarines, and because the German government was close to signing an anti-U.S. alliance with Mexico.

Led by large numbers of tanks, British troops capture German trenches in the first phase of the Battle of Cambrai, fought from late November until early December 1917. British gains were quickly lost due to rapid and strong German attacks.

GERMANY'S LAST GAMBLE

At the start of 1918 Germany was ruled as a military dictatorship with senior generals making all the real decisions. The head of the German army was Field Marshal Paul von Hindenburg, but the real boss was his senior assistant, General Erich Ludendorff. Germany was in a bad position at the start of 1918. Its enemies had been joined by the United States. American troops could be expected to reach the Western Front in the course of the year. The Germans planned one last decisive offensive before they arrived.

German troops move up to the front line prior to the opening of Germany's last great offensive on the Western Front. These men belong to one of the newly formed storm trooper units.

The American troops would not arrive in great numbers before the summer, however, and Ludendorff thought this gave him an opportunity. The Germans had defended successfully on the Western Front throughout 1916 and 1917 even though they had been outnumbered. Now, with Russia out of the war, they could switch troops from the Eastern Front and outnumber the British and French—at least until the Americans arrived in strength. It might have been better for Germany to have tried to make peace, but for a soldier like Ludendorff this was impossible. He wanted to attack and try to win the war.

STORM TROOPERS AND ARTILLERY TACTICS

Germany's attacks in 1918 employed new infantry and artillery tactics. Their artillery bombardments were short and concentrated on specific targets. The aim was to create a few gaps in the chain of defensive strongpoints and confuse the enemy commanders and artillery units. Most of the shells fired at enemy rear areas were gas shells. They did not aim to kill many enemy troops, but making the soldiers wear their gas masks was enough to make it very difficult for them to operate normally.

Specially trained infantry known as storm troopers then took up the attack. The first wave made no attempt to capture frontline enemy strongpoints. They slipped past them and cut them off. Follow-up troops would capture them later.

In the meantime the leading storm troopers could penetrate deeper and deeper into enemy territory. It was a tough tactic for the enemy to deal with. If the attack went according to plan, a huge gap could quickly be torn in the defenders' front lines.

Ludendorff correctly judged that the greatest weakness in the Allied forces was that they did not always work together well. The French would do everything they could to block a German advance toward Paris, but the British were more concerned to defend northern France and the ports on the English Channel that linked them to their homeland.

The road and rail communications between these northern areas and the rest of France passed through the city of Amiens. Ludendorff planned to attack Amiens and drive the British north and the French south. Once he had captured Amiens, the British and French would be unable to support each other, and he could then finish them off separately.

A series of offensives

It was an ambitious plan but Ludendorff had new tactics that might make it work. To make the breakthrough he needed, the German artillery would be assembled secretly and fire a short but fierce "hurricane" bombardment. Then specially trained storm trooper infantry would advance using infiltration tactics—bypassing enemy strongpoints and pushing deep behind the front line.

Training the new storm troopers revealed another German weakness that would become important later. A large number of German units had been so badly demoralized in the fighting of

With the imminent arrival of huge numbers of American troops, the German generals planned one final knockout blow to smash the Allies on the Western Front. The offensive initially went well, but the British and French fought back hard, eventually stopping the Germans in their tracks.

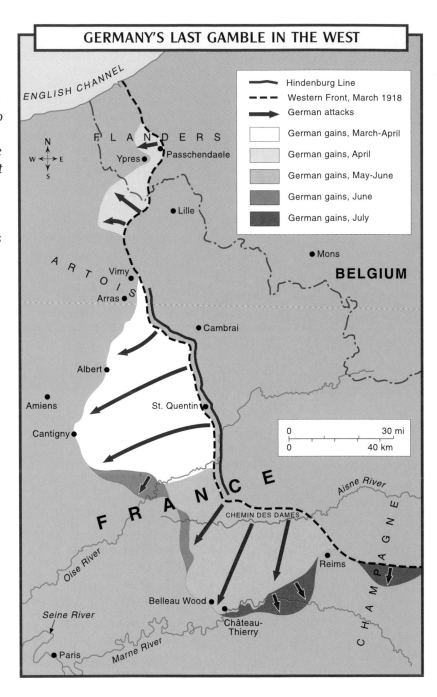

GERMANY'S LAST GAMBLE IN THE WEST

the previous year that they were not up to learning the new methods. Only a limited number of these storm troopers could be trained and, since they got the best rations and weapons, morale in the other units suffered even more. For most of the war the German army had held an advantage in fighting skill over its enemies, now only part of it still had the edge.

The German attack began on March 21, 1918, with a five-hour bombardment by almost 10,000 artillery guns and mortars. Three German armies faced two British along a 45-mile (72-km) front south of the town of Arras. Many of the British frontline positions were smashed by the German barrage, but the damage done to the British command centers and artillery positions was more important. Only some of these were knocked out, but most were made harmless by having their communications cut and their men prevented from moving by a rain of poison-gas shells.

By the end of the first day of the battle the British were in retreat and already had over 20,000 men taken prisoner. By March 25, the Germans had advanced about 25 miles (40 km), farther and faster than in any Western Front battle since 1914. It seemed as if Ludendorff's grand strategy was working, too, for Pétain, the French commander-in-chief, was refusing to send any significant help to the British.

Renewed German attacks

In fact, Ludendorff's plan was beginning to fall apart. On March 26, the British and French governments appointed General Ferdinand Foch to coordinate their operations on the Western Front and supervise their national commanders, Field Marshal Douglas Haig and General Henri Pétain. From then on the Allies worked together much more effectively. Although the German attacks were still gaining ground, their advance was being stopped in the most vital sector near Amiens.

By early April Ludendorff knew that further efforts were useless, and he halted the offensive on the 5th. Both sides had about 250,000 casualties, but these were casualties that the Germans in particular could ill afford.

Within a few days, Ludendorff was ready to begin a new attack, this time around the city of Ypres in the northern, British-held sector of the front. The attack began on April 9 with the same tactics as

British and French troops man a new trench line after being forced back by the Germans during the opening stage of their great offensive on the Western Front in March 1918.

German storm troopers cross over the shell-blasted area between the rival trenches during the opening phase of their offensive. Early gains were spectacular, but the attacking troops failed to take full advantage of their success.

before. Again, some parts of the Allied front line were broken, but once again the desperate Allied defense halted the German advance within a few days.

Ludendorff was not yet finished, however. He knew that the British were still his toughest opponents, but he could not attack them again until he had drawn some of the Allied reserves off to the south. He switched his artillery and his remaining storm troopers south to the Chemin des Dames area of the Aisne River sector. The hurricane bombardment crashed out once again on May 27. The local French commander, General Louis Franchet d'Esperey, made a mess of his defensive plans, and the Allies were defeated along a 25-mile (40-km) front.

The Americans arrive

By the end of May the German attacks had gained another 30 miles (48 km) of ground. They had reached the Marne River at Château-Thierry and seemed poised to drive on toward Paris to win the war. It was not to be, for their troops were exhausted and Allied reserves were in position to counterattack.

For the first time American troops played a significant part in the fighting. The United States had entered the war on April 6, 1917. General John Pershing was placed in command of the troops earmarked for Europe, the American Expeditionary Force (A.E.F.). The first Americans arrived in Europe in June 1917, but Pershing planned to have one million troops by May 1918.

Pershing's U.S. troops first fought battles at Cantigny, Château-Thierry, and Belleau Wood during late May and June 1918. At Cantigny the U.S. First Division captured the German-held village and then held off desperate German counterattacks. At Château-Thierry the U.S. Third Division halted the German advance across the Marne and then threw the Germans back. The U.S. Second Division, mainly composed of U.S. Marines, suffered over 50 percent casualties but helped halt the Germans and then drove them back in the Battle of Belleau Wood in early June. Ludendorff halted the German attacks on June 4.

Ludendorff knew he had to keep attacking to keep the advantage, but many of his trained storm troopers had been killed in his three earlier offensives. Their replacements were inexperienced and less aggressive in battle and most German infantry units were now badly understrength. Despite this shortage of top-quality troops, he ordered two more German attacks.

Each of these attacks suffered the same fate, winning ground for the first two or three days before being halted by the Allies. Even worse for the Germans was the fact that the Allies were able to halt these attacks without committing all their reserves. Foch now planned a series of offensives to drive the Germans back once and for all. A great deal of hard fighting remained to complete the Allied victory on the Western Front, but Germany had now definitely lost the war.

U.S. troops, probably members of the Third Division, in action during the Battle of Château-Thierry. They were able to halt the dangerous German advance across the Marne River.

THE ALLIES HIT BACK

The first six months of 1918 had seen crisis after crisis for the Allied armies in France as the German attacks bit deep into their lines. By July, however, the tide had turned. Each side had lost at least half a million men in the battles of the first half of the year, but the Allies had brought new troops to France from Britain and from other war theaters, and their forces were being boosted even more by the arrival of 300,000 fresh Americans every month. The war on the Western Front was entering its final phase.

U.S. troops board the trucks that will take them up to the front prior to the opening of their offensive against the Germans in the Second Battle of the Marne, July 1918.

General Erich Ludendorff's fifth great offensive of the year gave the Allies their cue to take the initiative. The German attack, known as the Second Battle of the Marne, began on July 15. Ludendorff planned to advance on two fronts, east and west of the city of Reims (see map page 62), but good Allied intelligence and clever defensive tactics meant that the attack east of the city was halted before it could get going. West of the city the Germans did better and managed to push a large force across the Marne River. Within two days, however, they had been fought to a standstill by the French, helped by American troops.

Ludendorff now realized that his men were exposed and vulnerable in the great salient, or bulge, his last three attacks had made in the front line. Unfortunately for the Germans the Allied leaders had spotted this weakness, too, and were themselves ready to attack, before the Germans could pull back from the salient. The Allied advance began on July 18 and the assault smashed into the German right flank. Most of the attacking troops were from the French Tenth and Sixth Armies, but these formations included American, British, and Italian units as well as French. The U.S. First and Second Divisions spearheaded the French Tenth Army attack.

The attack was supported by 2,000 artillery guns, 1,200 aircraft, and over 500 tanks. These weapons helped the advance gain almost eight miles (13 km) of ground on the first day. By the time the Allied generals halted their drive to reorganize their forces at the start of August, all the territory the Germans had captured in the Aisne and Marne sectors in May and June had been retaken.

Germany on the retreat

Six other American divisions as well as the First and Second gained some battle experience alongside the French in the course of this fighting, but this was a departure from the usual American policy during the war. General Pershing had been instructed by his government to keep his units together as a single all-American formation, and not to put American troops under the command of a foreign general.

Strictly speaking, the United States was only an "associated power" in the war against Germany and had no formal alliance with either Britain or France. Pershing was accordingly told to cooperate with the other Allied armies on the Western Front but to keep his forces independent. During the Marne fighting Marshal Ferdinand Foch finally agreed that the U.S. forces in France would be allocated their own sector of the front line, at St. Mihiel, where Pershing would fight his first large-scale battle in September.

In the meantime other Allied forces were ready to increase the pressure on the Germans. After the mainly French victories of July, the British were ready to take over the lead in the Allied efforts in August. The British Fourth Army was secretly reinforced and began a crushing attack in the Battle of Amiens in the Somme sector on August 8. Like all Allied attacks from then on,

GENERAL JOHN PERSHING

General Pershing, commander of U.S. troops in France.

General John Pershing commanded the U.S. forces in France throughout 1917 and 1918. Before World War I Pershing had seen service in Cuba and the Philippines and commanded the U.S. invasion of Mexico in 1916–17.

As soon as American troops began arriving in France, the British and French tried to persuade Pershing to split his forces up to reinforce different parts of the Allied lines. Pershing would have none of it. He did allow some of his units to be committed to help block the German drives in the Marne River sector in June and July 1918, but otherwise he insisted that American troops must fight as a single, united force. Because organizing this took so long, it was not until the attack at St. Mihiel in September that American troops fought any big battles.

Pershing's determination to do things his own way also meant that he did not learn as much as he could have from the experience and methods of the British and French. This was one of the causes of the behind-the-lines problems that slowed the American advance during the offensive in the final weeks of the war. Pershing's mistakes may have gotten the U.S. Army into difficulties, but he quickly made changes that would have improved matters if the war had gone on any longer.

it relied on a combination of infantry, artillery, tanks, and aircraft to smash through the German lines. The Germans were taken by surprise and pushed back as much as eight miles (13 km) along the 20-mile (32-km) attack front on the first day.

General Erich Ludendorff was dismayed to learn that some of his frontline forces had panicked or surrendered as soon as they could. The British kept their advance going for almost a week, but day by day their progress slowed down. The tanks had played a big part in the initial success but only six of the 414 used on the first day were still fit for action by August 12. Many had been knocked out by German artillery fire, but more had simply broken down or gotten stuck in difficult ground.

A new Allied strategy

Both sides had now devised good tactics that made it possible to break through a tough enemy defense line. The Germans used hurricane artillery bombardments and infantry infiltration tactics, while the Allies had added tanks and strong air forces to their similar infantry and artillery techniques. However, the Allies were now discovering what the Germans had found earlier in 1918— breaking through was one thing, but taking advantage of a success was another. Neither side had reliable tanks or other fighting vehicles capable of bursting through the initial gap torn in enemy lines to turn an advance into an overwhelming victory.

In 1916 and 1917 Field Marshal Douglas Haig and other Allied generals had been criticized for continuing with offensives for months, long after any momentum had been lost. Now they

German prisoners look on as their own and British medical staff treat casualties of the fighting in the summer of 1918.

The U.S.-led offensive at St. Mihiel in 1918 was a joint attack by U.S. and French forces. The aim was to smash through a bulge in the German front line. The attack was successful with 15,000 German prisoners taken. American casualties amounted to 7,000.

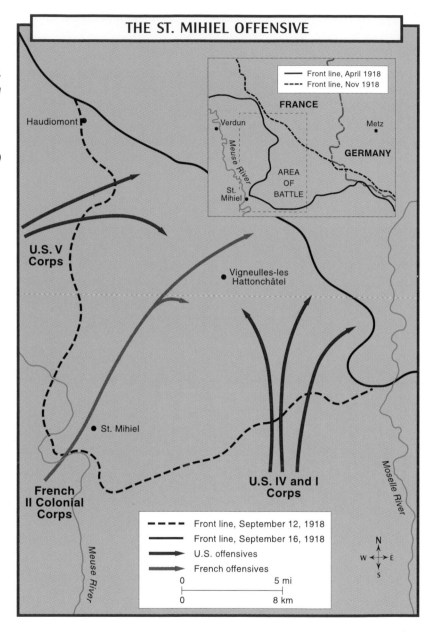

THE ST. MIHIEL OFFENSIVE

—— Front line, April 1918
---- Front line, Nov 1918

FRANCE

Verdun

Metz

Meuse River

GERMANY

St. Mihiel

AREA OF BATTLE

Haudiomont

U.S. V Corps

Vigneulles-les Hattonchâtel

St. Mihiel

French II Colonial Corps

U.S. IV and I Corps

Moselle River

---- Front line, September 12, 1918
—— Front line, September 16, 1918
→ U.S. offensives
→ French offensives

Meuse River

N
W ← → E
S

0   5 mi
0   8 km

tried a different and more effective strategy. On August 15, they decided to halt their advance east of Amiens and switched their efforts farther north.

The British Third Army attacked successfully in this area between August 21–29, and then the First Army took over the lead farther north still at the end of August. Haig and Foch had both realized that by constantly switching the point of their attacks in this way they could keep the Germans retreating. By early September the Germans had decided that the bulge in their lines around the town of St. Mihiel on the Meuse River was likely to be attacked by the Allies.

The Germans decided to pull out, but they were too late. On September 12 the U.S. First Army, led by General Pershing, attacked with some 300,000 men. By September 16, when the battle ended, the whole of the bulge in the German line had been captured along with 15,000 German prisoners, at a cost of fewer than 7,000 American casualties.

A key victory

We now know that it was an easier victory than it seemed at the time, because the Germans were caught halfway through their withdrawal and in no condition to put up a real fight, but the success was a great boost to the morale of the American troops.

By mid-September the Allied advance all along the front had regained all the ground the Germans had won in the first half of the year, and more in areas like St. Mihiel. The Germans had fallen back to the Hindenburg Line, the toughest defenses built by either side in the whole war. The Allies were now on top in the war, but if the Germans could defeat their attacks on the Hindenburg Line, Germany might still be able to fight on.

An American rifleman opens fire on a German position amid the ruins of a French village during the fighting around St. Mihiel in the middle of September 1918.

U.S. PRESSURE COUNTS

The Meuse–Argonne offensive began on September 26, 1918, and continued until the armistice that ended the war on November 11. It was one of a series of simultaneous offensives by the Allied forces that drove the Germans back all along the front line in France. On the Allied side, the Meuse–Argonne battle was mainly fought by the U.S. First Army, with some French support. It was the largest battle fought by American troops during World War I.

An American gun mounted on a rail truck opens fire on German positions during the Meuse–Argonne offensive on the Western Front.

The objective of the attack was to advance northward along a 30-mile (48-km) front to the west of the town of Verdun, and cut a railroad line running through Sedan and Mézières in eastern France that was vital to the German supply system. To reach this objective the U.S. forces would have to advance 40 miles (64 km) or more through difficult and well-defended territory.

The Argonne Forest, an area of steep slopes and tree-covered ridges, largely blocked the path of the offensive. The forest was pierced by a number of river valleys, including that of the Meuse, but the valleys were narrow and guarded by carefully constructed and elaborate German defenses. Even getting ready for the attack was a tough challenge for the American forces for many of them were still fighting in the St. Mihiel battle off to the southwest as late as September 16.

A crucial battle

This new offensive would be the first mainly American battle of the war and would be a key test to see if Pershing's policy of keeping his own forces separate from those of France and Britain and under his direct command was correct. Some British and French generals believed that the U.S. units in France should be placed under their leadership, but this was a view that Pershing and leading U.S. politicians opposed. The Argonne attack would also show the value of the combat experience the U.S. forces in France had gained in their earlier battles.

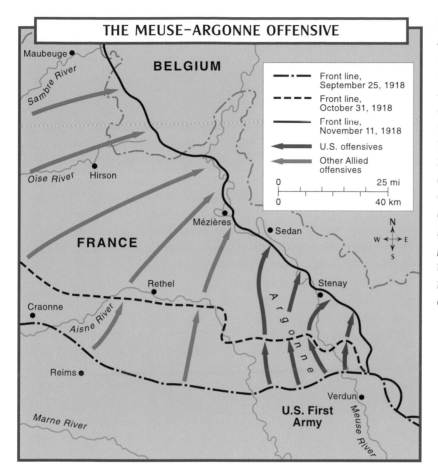

THE MEUSE–ARGONNE OFFENSIVE

Maubeuge

BELGIUM

Sambre River

Oise River   Hirson

FRANCE

Mézières

Sedan

Rethel

Stenay

Craonne

Aisne River

Argonne

Reims

Verdun

U.S. First
Army

Marne River

Meuse River

— ·— Front line, September 25, 1918

— — — Front line, October 31, 1918

——— Front line, November 11, 1918

◄— U.S. offensives

◄— Other Allied offensives

0 ___ 25 mi
0 ___ 40 km

N
W — E
S

The U.S. attack in the Argonne Forest sector of the Western Front began on September 26. The Argonne was a key point in the German defenses on the Western Front. At first progress was slow due to stubborn German resistance and difficult terrain. However, the advance picked up speed, and the Germans were in full retreat by the end of October.

The Germans would certainly try to make things as tough as they could for the newcomers. If the offensive failed, the American people's wholehearted enthusiasm for the war might be blunted, and the Germans could hope for a more favorable treaty to end the war. There was a lot at stake.

The offensive stalls

About 600,000 Allied troops participated in the offensive at first. These were mainly from General Hunter Liggett's U.S. First Army with support from General Henri Gouraud's French Fourth Army. The attack was backed by some 5,000 artillery guns, over 500 tanks, and a strong force of aircraft. These helped ensure that the first day of the battle was successful. The Allied forces advanced up to three miles (5 km) into German-held territory and took over 20,000 German troops prisoner.

73

AFRICAN AMERICANS IN WORLD WAR I

World War I had a major impact on the distribution of African Americans across the United States. Shortages of labor in arms factories in the northern states led many rural African Americans to travel north in search of work. They played a vital role in making the weapons and equipment needed by the U.S. forces fighting in France.

African Americans also fought in World War I. Over 400,000 volunteered for service, and African Americans made up 13 percent of the soldiers of the American Expeditionary Force fighting in France. African Americans, however, fought in segregated units, usually officered by whites, and frequently received less than fair treatment. They were often forced to do the most menial, low-grade jobs, despite widespread evidence that African American units could fight well. Many instances of battlefield bravery were recorded, but no African American soldier received the Congressional Medal of Honor for his role in the war.

One African American soldier, James Reese Europe of the 369th U.S. Infantry Regiment, was a noted jazz musician and composer, who used his frontline experience to write songs such as "On Patrol in No-Man's-Land" and "All of No-Man's-Land is Ours."

Then things began to go wrong. The difficult terrain and tough German defenses made it essential that the follow-up attacks work to a carefully coordinated artillery and infantry plan, but the troops were too inexperienced to do this quickly. Artillery units fell behind the advancing infantry or took too long to zero in on new targets. The result was that some infantry attacks went in without proper support and took heavy casualties.

Pershing tried to send in reserves to get the advance going properly, but this only made matters worse. There was only a handful of roads leading into the battle area, and these were soon completely gridlocked. Many of the reserves did not get into battle, and some frontline units were left without food or ammunition. By September 30, the attacks had gained about 10 miles (16 km) of ground in some places, but then they had to be halted.

Problems like these were probably unavoidable. Staff officers and commanders were having to learn their business as they went along. Pershing was not one of the most brilliant generals of the war, but he was quick to fire incompetent officers and promote better ones in their place. It was harsh, but it made the A.E.F. a better fighting force.

The final breakthrough

The second phase of the attack started on October 4, with a greater proportion of the frontline troops now being made up of veterans of the St. Mihiel battle. The German defenses were so tough that progress was still very slow. The terrain meant that there was often no other option than to batter straight ahead.

Some French leaders thought this slow progress was Pershing's fault and tried to get him fired but Foch supported Pershing and he kept his job. In addition to the organizational changes he made in the First Army, Pershing set up the U.S. Second Army in France during October but it was not ready until a few days before the end of the war in November.

By the end of October the American attack had finally penetrated through the Argonne Forest into more open country. Pershing sent fresh troops forward to lead a renewed advance, and at last the German front began to crack. By the time the war came to an end on November 11, most of the objectives for the offensive had finally been reached. It had been a costly process, however, with 117,000 American casualties, almost half of America's total losses for the whole war.

African American troops move to the front line in the Argonne Forest, November 1918.

THE FINAL OFFENSIVE

By late September 1918 the Allied armies were ready to begin their final advances to win the war. The U.S. First Army's attack in the Meuse–Argonne region was only one of four powerful Allied drives. The British attacked east of Ypres and farther south near St. Quentin, while the French pushed forward in the Champagne region. These massive attacks swept all before them while the German forces collapsed and thousands of troops surrendered as the Allies drove forward.

The British and French attacks started on September 27 and it was the British forces that struck the decisive blow. By then the German armies had retreated to their old Hindenburg Line defenses and General Erich Ludendorff hoped to hold out there long enough to convince the Allies to agree to a peace treaty favorable to Germany. He was shocked when carefully planned British attacks, led by Canadian and Australian troops, smashed through the Hindenburg Line in three days.

An end in sight

From then until the end of the war in November, there were few spectacular big battles, but a continuous series of smaller advances by the Allied forces. German machine-gun troops often put up a tough fight and caused many casualties, but many more German troops had had enough and either surrendered to the Allies or deserted from their army.

The scale of the German defeat in late summer 1918 is reflected in this haul of prisoners. By fall 1918, the morale of many German soldiers on the Western Front was at rock bottom, and most were eager to surrender.

Germany and its allies had now lost the war. Bulgaria stopped fighting at the end of September, Turkey gave up at the end of October, and by early November the Austro-Hungarian Empire was falling apart. Peace negotiations between Germany and the Allies actually started in late September but into October the Germans still tried to insist on a deal that allowed them to hold on to captured territory in Eastern Europe.

The reality was that Germany had no choice. Without allies, and with strikes and antiwar protests at home turning into revolution, the outlook was grim. But the main reason for Germany's problems was that the German army had been thoroughly defeated in battle, even though its leaders did not want to admit it.

The German army's plans had been instrumental in starting the war in 1914. Germany's generals had virtually ruled their country for most of the war and had insisted on achieving an outright military victory, whatever it might cost, ignoring opportunities for a negotiated peace that would have benefited the German people. This strategy had failed and the Allies were poised to overrun Germany, if not in late 1918 then in 1919.

A new civilian government took over in Germany in early October. Ludendorff resigned from his post as Germany's chief military planner on October 27 and this cleared the way for the German government to agree finally with the Allies on an end to the fighting. The armistice came into effect at 11:00 A.M. on November 11, 1918.

Counting the cost

Strictly speaking an armistice was only a temporary end to the war to see if a peace treaty could be agreed upon, but the fighting was over for good. The Treaty of Versailles and other agreements that ended the war were completed during 1919.

People in all countries hoped that World War I would be the "war to end all wars." The human cost had been horrendous; about ten million soldiers and sailors had been killed in the fighting and at least another seven million civilians had died because of the war. Many more had been permanently crippled by their wounds or been mentally traumatized by their suffering or the loss of their loved ones. However, their hopes for a permanent peace would also be dashed. When World War II began in Europe in 1939, it had generally similar causes to World War I and would be fought by more or less the same countries. World War I had solved nothing.

Representatives from the major powers in World War I prepare to sign the Treaty of Versailles in 1919, ending the conflict. The conference was chaired by U.S. President Woodrow Wilson, who hoped to secure a settlement that would provide a framework for peace in Europe. Despite his best intentions, there was to be no long-lasting peace. Europe, and later the world, would again be at war 20 years later.

GLOSSARY

airship A gas-filled balloon based on a rigid metal structure. In World War I airships were used for long-range bombing, reconnaissance, and protecting convoys from submarine attack.

barrage A usually long-lasting artillery bombardment, which often heralds an offensive. A barrage aims to kill enemy troops, smash fortifications, and destroy an opponent's artillery.

blockade A form of naval strategy. Its aim is not chiefly to destroy an enemy's fleet but keep it bottled up in harbor, and prevent an enemy's merchant fleet from sailing. An enemy would eventually run out of the resources, such as food and raw materials, to continue fighting.

convoy A means of protecting a large number of merchant ships from enemy submarine attack. The vessels sailed in several parallel lines protected by a screen of warships carrying weapons designed to sink submarines.

defense in depth A term referring to a defensive system that consists of line upon line of trenches or other fortifications. The idea was that an enemy attack might capture one or two of these defensive lines, but would be so disorganized or suffer such high casualties that the remaining defensive lines would be able to defeat the attack.

dreadnought A fast, heavily armed, and heavily armored battleship. The first was launched by the British in 1906 and easily outclassed any other battleships in existence.

pillbox A type of small fortification, usually built out of concrete or steel, and holding a handful of men. Small, strong, and hard to spot, pillboxes were difficult to destroy. Troops inside a pillbox often manned a machine gun and could easily halt an enemy attack, even one in large numbers.

reserves Troops held back from the opening of an attack. They are usually thrown into a battle to exploit any advantage won in the first stages of an offensive or to block any enemy successes.

tank A tracked vehicle covered in armor and fitted with either cannon or machine guns or a mixture of both. The first tanks were slow and underpowered. When they were being developed in great secrecy by the British in World War I, they were described in documents as water tanks to mislead the enemy, hence their name.

trench A deep, narrow, often zigzagging defensive position dug into the earth and protected by barbed wire. Trenches also had deep shell-proof shelters where troops could take cover from enemy artillery fire.

BIBLIOGRAPHY

Note: *An asterisk (*) denotes a Young Adult title.*

*Brownstone, David and Franck, Irene. *Timelines of Warfare From 100,000 B.C. to the Present*. Little, Brown and Company, 1994.

Ferro, Marc. *The Great War, 1914–1918*. Routledge, 1997

*Griffiths, Paddy. *Battle Tactics on the Western Front, 1916–1918*. Yale University Press, 1994.

Halpern, Paul G. *A Naval History of World War I*. United States Naval Institute, 1994.

*Keegan, John, and Wheatcroft, Andrew. *Who's Who in Military History: 1453 to the Present Day*. Routledge, 1998.

Joll, James. *The Origins of the First World War*. Addison Wesley Longman, 1998.

*Macdonald, Lyn, *1914–1918: Voices and Images of the Great War*. Penguin Books USA, Inc., 1991.

Smith, Gene. *Until the Last Trumpet Sounds— The Life of General of the Armies John J. Pershing*. John Wiley & Sons, Inc., 1998

Stone, Norman. *The Eastern Front, 1914–1917*. Penguin Putnam Inc., 1998.

INDEX

ACKNOWLEDGMENTS

Cover (main picture) Robert Hunt Library, (inset) Peter Newark's Military Pictures; page 1 Peter Newark's Military Pictures; page 5 Robert Hunt Library; page 6 Robert Hunt Library; page 7 Robert Hunt Library; page 8 Robert Hunt Library; page 10 Peter Newark's Military Pictures; page 12 Robert Hunt Library; page 13 Robert Hunt Library; page 14 Robert Hunt Library; page 16 Robert Hunt Library; page 17 Robert Hunt Library; page 18 Robert Hunt Library; page 20 Robert Hunt Library; page 22 Robert Hunt Library; page 24 Robert Hunt Library; page 27 Robert Hunt Library; page 28 Robert Hunt Library; page 30 Robert Hunt Library; page 32 Robert Hunt Library; page 33 Robert Hunt Library; page 34 Robert Hunt Library; page 36 Robert Hunt Library; page 37 AKG Photo, London; page 38 Robert Hunt Library; page 41 AKG Photo, London; page 43 Robert Hunt Library; page 44 Robert Hunt Library; page 46 Robert Hunt Library; page 48 Robert Hunt Library; page 50 Peter Newark's Military Pictures; page 52 Robert Hunt Library; page 53 AKG Photo, London/Eric Lessing; page 54 Peter Newark's Pictures; page 56 Robert Hunt Library; page 59 Peter Newark's Military Pictures; page 60 Robert Hunt Library; page 63 Robert Hunt Librarys; page 64 Robert Hunt Library; page 65 Peter Newark's Military Pictures; page 66 Robert Hunt Library; page 68 Robert Hunt Library; page 69 Robert Hunt Library; page 71 Peter Newark's Military Pictures; page 72 Robert Hunt Library; page 75 Robert Hunt Library; page 76 Robert Hunt Library; page 77 Peter Newark's Military Pictures.